"*Testosterone for Life* provides the science an
behind the safe and effective use of testosterone therapy in
men with low levels of testosterone. Dr. Morgentaler is an
internationally recognized expert in sexual medicine and
andrology (male hormones). In this book he shares his secrets
for a healthy life in a way the lay reader can both understand
and appreciate. This is a 'must-read' book for men of all ages and
the women who care about them."

—*Irwin Goldstein, M.D.*
Director of Sexual Medicine, Alvarado Hospital, San Diego
Editor-in-Chief, Journal of Sexual Medicine

"*Testosterone for Life* is yet another great contribution to
men's health literature by Dr. Morgentaler. An intriguing
combination of maverick and Harvard physician/scientist, he
flips conventional medical thought on its head by debunking
many of the long-standing myths about testosterone, including
the controversial link between testosterone therapy and prostate
cancer. Dr. Morgentaler has written an authoritative book that
is easy to read and that will serve as an invaluable resource to
both men and their physicians."

—*Philip Kantoff, M.D.*
Director of Lank Center for Genitourinary Oncology,
Dana Farber Cancer Institute

"A highly valuable resource that finally debunks many of the myths about testosterone's safety, which has been an impediment to its appropriate usage for far too long."

—David E. Greenberg, M.D.
President, Canadian Society for the Study of the Aging Male

"With *Testosterone for Life*, Dr. Morgentaler provides women the tools and clear information they need to determine if their male partners' low libido is a result of normal aging, relationship woes, or a real and treatable medical condition. Dr. Morgentaler has been a powerful and outspoken advocate for improved sexual intimacy and healthy living, and, in this book, he shows how treatment of low testosterone can restore vitality in men and potentially rejuvenate floundering relationships."

—Laura Berman, LCSW, Ph.D.
Author of Real Sex for Real Women

Testosterone for Life

Recharge Your Vitality, Sex Drive, Muscle Mass & Overall Health!

ABRAHAM MORGENTALER, M.D.
Associate Clinical Professor, Harvard Medical School

New York   Chicago   San Francisco   Lisbon   London   Madrid   Mexico City
Milan   New Delhi   San Juan   Seoul   Singapore   Sydney   Toronto

Library of Congress Cataloging-in-Publication Data

Morgentaler, Abraham.
    Testosterone for life : recharge your vitality, sex drive, muscle mass, and overall health / by Abraham Morgentaler.
        p.   cm.
    ISBN 978-0-07-149480-9 (alk. paper)
    1. Testosterone—Popular works.   2. Men—Health and hygiene—Popular works.   I. Title.

QP572.T4.M67   2009
612.6′1—dc22   2008034610

9 10 11 12 13 14 15 16 17 18 19 20 21 22 23   DOC/DOC 1 5 4 3 2

ISBN   978-0-07-149480-9
MHID   0-07-149480-4

Figure on page 27 by Alex Gonzalez; figures on pages 25, 33, 62, 96 by Scott Leighton

McGraw-Hill books are available at special quantity discounts to use as premiums and sales promotions or for use in corporate training programs. To contact a representative, please visit the Contact Us pages at www.mhprofessional.com.

The information contained in this book is intended to provide helpful and informative material on the subject addressed. It is not intended to serve as a replacement for professional medical advice. Any use of the information in this book is at the reader's discretion. The author, publisher, and the President and Fellows of Harvard University specifically disclaim any and all liability arising directly or indirectly from the use or application of any information contained in this book. A health-care professional should be consulted regarding your specific situation.

This book is printed on acid-free paper.

This book is dedicated to my teachers: to Bahadur Bhatla, my high school science teacher who nourished the science spark in me; to Dr. David Crews, for introducing me to the world of testosterone and investigative thought; to Reuben Gittes, M.D., for inspiring me to question everything; and to William DeWolf, M.D., my mentor and intellectual sounding board, for his unfailing support and encouragement.

Contents

Contents

Acknowledgments

This book represents my best effort to provide a much-needed book on testosterone for the millions of men with low T who are without a solid source of reliable information. It has also been an opportunity for me to present the evolution of my own thoughts and perspectives on this topic, which have developed over much of my adult life. I am grateful to many individuals both for their contributions to the publication of this book and for their contributions to me.

First and foremost, I wish to thank Anthony Komaroff, M.D., at Harvard Health Publications, for his willingness to even consider a book of this nature and then for making it happen. Johanna Bowman at McGraw-Hill has been an outstanding editor, and I am grateful for her clarity of thought, for her helping me figure out what is important (and unimportant) to say, and for her willingness to abide my sense of humor. A very big thank-you to Julie Silver, M.D., at Harvard Health Publications for helping me find and trust my own voice in this book—that was huge! Thanks as well to Raquel Schott for organizing the illustrations, to Scott Leighton for his outstanding artwork, and to Julia Anderson Bauer and Judith McCarthy at McGraw-Hill for pulling everything together.

My perspectives on testosterone have been developed over thirty years, and I have been extremely fortunate in my life to have shared space with so many creative and brilliant minds from around the world, teaching me, challenging me, inspiring me. I am indebted to them all. As I am certain to inadvertently omit a great many individuals if I even attempt to include them all, let me instead simply mention a few. Particular thanks go to Andy Guay, M.D., and Abdul Traish, Ph.D., for sharing so many hours passionately discussing aspects of testosterone. Many thanks as well to Shally Bhasin, M.D., the "Dean of Testosterone," for his graciousness in inviting my comments and opinions in a number of educational settings. A special word of appreciation and admiration to Irwin Goldstein, M.D., for the inspirational way he has led the field of sexual medicine for the last twenty years and for his enthusiastic support of my work, as well as the work of so many others. A word of appreciation as well to Bruno Lunenfeld, M.D., for his international efforts to raise awareness of the importance of low testosterone to aging men.

Ideas do not usually appear by themselves, fully formed. Coherent new concepts require discussion, criticism, counterargument, pushback, perspective, wisdom, and experience. In this regard, I am indebted to many conversations and interactions with a number of accomplished individuals and luminaries—Ray Rosen, Ph.D.; Ricardo Munarriz, M.D.; Ridwan Shabsigh, M.D.; Han Hanafy, M.D.; Leonard Marks, M.D.; Jacob Rajfer, M.D.; David Crawford, M.D.; Ian Thompson, M.D.; Culley Carson, M.D.; John Morley, M.D.; Paul Lange, M.D.; Sanjeev Vohra, M.D.; Carl Bruning, M.D.; Kevin Khoudray, M.D.; Martin Miner, M.D.; Larry Lipshultz, M.D.; Steve Lazarou, M.D.; Paul Church, M.D.; Ron Swerdloff, M.D.; Christina Wang, M.D.; Lisa Tenover, M.D.; Al Matsumoto, M.D.; Adrian Dobs, M.D.; Bill Bremner, M.D.; John McKinlay, Ph.D.; Andre Araujo, Ph.D.; Laurence Levine, M.D.; and Glenn Cunningham, M.D. We may not have always agreed, but I always benefited from our discussions. Glenn Bubley, M.D., Phil Kantoff, M.D., and Marc Garnick, M.D., all accomplished experts themselves in the field of prostate cancer, have graciously indulged my frequent questions and occasionally inflammatory comments regarding testosterone and prostate cancer over the years—thank you.

Around the world, I am deeply indebted to Ernani Rhoden, M.D., in Brazil, for his hard work and his great mind and for elevating the quality of our collaborative testosterone research. Thanks as well to Luis Reyes-Vallejo, M.D., in Mexico, for his great spirit, and to Farid Saad, M.D.; Aksam Yassim, M.D.; and Claude Schulman, M.D., as they circle the globe, for feeding me the latest interesting testosterone research papers via the Internet.

Bill DeWolf, M.D., has provided me with everything one could wish from a mentor—in particular, encouragement for the most ambitious ideas combined with a grounded skepticism that has forced me to become more rigorous and disciplined in my arguments. A special thank-you to Mike Schopperle, Ph.D., one of the finest scientific minds I know, for all the late-night brainstorming sessions doodling ideas on paper napkins over a couple of beers.

Many thanks to my office staff—Kerry and Randy Eaton, Vikki Zdanovich, Madeleine Mackell, and Orville Williams—for creating a great environment where the actual work with men with low T takes place. A very special and heartfelt thanks to Kevin Flinn, R.N., my right-hand man and loyal fellow warrior in the "testosterone wars" over the last fifteen-plus years.

Many thanks to my mother, Dr. Chawa Rosenfarb; my father, Henry Morgentaler, M.D.; and to my sister, Dr. Goldie Morgentaler and her husband, Dr. Jonathan Seldin, for their love and support. It would have been impossible for me to write a book about living well without the help of my two beautiful daughters, Maya and Hanni, who have always helped me see what is important in life, and my fiancée, Mo Keovongsa, who has given me the space to write, work, and pursue my dreams while always letting me know there was a warm, loving space for me to come home to.

Finally, a word of gratitude to my patients, who have entrusted me with their stories and their health. Thank you for sharing your lives with me and for teaching me so much. I hope this book does justice to your faith in me.

Introduction

Are you tired? Have you lost your edge, your sense of vitality, your "mojo"? Does sex feel like work, or maybe it doesn't work out anymore? Is your mood blah?" Have you put on a gut even though you don't seem to be eating any more than you ever did? Maybe it's age. Or maybe, just maybe, you have a medical condition called low testosterone, or, as I prefer to call it, low T.

If you do, you should know that treatment of low T has an excellent chance of helping you feel better. Not only do many men experience improvement in their sexual function and return of their old desire for sex, but they also say they feel like their battery has been recharged. They say they feel younger, more vigorous, or "the best I've felt in years!"

What's more, low T is incredibly common. Testosterone levels decline as we age, beginning around thirty-five years of age. By the time a man is seventy years old, there is a 50 percent chance that his T levels will be lower than the lowest values seen for men in their twenties. In men who have diabetes, obesity, hypertension, or lung disease, the risk of having low T approaches one in three for men over the age of forty.

Yet here's the crazy thing. For the longest time, despite recognizing the symptoms of low T for centuries, very few doctors offered treatment. The diagnosis and treatment have been part of all standard medical textbooks for several decades, yet there has been a great deal of confusion and a lack of clear guidelines about how to diagnose and how to treat low T. For the average man in reasonable health who feels his internal battery has worn down, this has meant that no one, including his own physician, has likely gone to the trouble of determining whether he might have low T.

Every week, I see men in my office who come in with classic symptoms and test results for low T, but whose physicians have either dismissed their complaints ("Joe, you just need to accept you're getting older.") or misinterpreted the test results ("That's strange—you have all the symptoms of low T, but this report says your testosterone levels are normal. I guess that's not it."). In other cases, the doctor has made the right diagnosis but just didn't feel comfortable prescribing testosterone therapy.

It doesn't have to be that way. As a urologist at Harvard Medical School, I've been treating men with low T for the last twenty years. When I include my undergraduate research at Harvard College on the effects of testosterone and other hormones on the brain, then I've been at this work for thirty years. It's what I do. And I've written this book to provide clear and helpful information so that men can be empowered to determine for themselves whether they have low T and, if so, whether they are interested in a trial of treatment.

Even after all these years of working with men with low T, I continue to be amazed at the ways in which T therapy can absolutely change a man's life. Not long ago, I saw Justin (all patient names have been changed for privacy reasons) in the office one year after he began testosterone treatment. As a fifty-two-year-old man, his original symptoms had been limited to reduced sexual desire. Otherwise, he told me during his initial visit, he felt perfectly fine.

"How have you been, Justin?" I asked as we sat down at his follow-up visit.

"Doctor," he began, "as you predicted, my sex drive came back quickly. What I hadn't expected, though, was how much better I would feel in other ways. In retrospect, I'd lost my zest for life, but I didn't realize it at the time because it had happened so gradually. Within a couple of months of treatment, I felt better than I'd felt in years. I'd always been creative in business, but I had let everything slip. In the last six months, I've started two new businesses, and I'm helping a colleague with the creation of a nonprofit educational company. I'm now excited to wake up every single day."

I hear stories like Justin's all the time. As a rule, guys don't like to go to the doctor; when they do, it's usually to treat some specific problem that won't go away. Most men I see come in for a specific issue, such as problems with erections or reduced sex drive. Testosterone therapy can be extremely helpful for these symptoms, yet in many ways the most important benefits of T therapy is the feeling of being "recharged" again—feeling more focused, more vigorous, more masculine, more alive.

It's really no wonder that many physicians are uncertain about their obligation to treat something like this. After all, no one dies from feeling run down or from having less sex drive. But it's a lousy way to go through life. And if symptoms can be relieved safely and effectively, then why not get treatment?

Augustino's story provides a slightly different perspective on the benefits of T therapy. Augustino is a distinguished professor of political science at one of the prestigious universities in the Boston area, who was unsure why he had been referred to me. "I'm not certain my problem is in the field of urology," he said, "but my regular doctor referred me to you because he thought I might have low testosterone. The thing that disturbs me most is that my brain doesn't seem as sharp as it should be. And for the last year or so, I feel like I'm just pushing time, going through my daily routine without any excitement. Since my whole life is dependent on being curious and mentally sharp, I'd be grateful if there was something you could do to help me."

The professor's blood tests revealed low T, and I started him on therapy. At three months he came back for his follow-up visit. He jumped up when I entered the room, with a big smile on his face, and clasped my hand in both of his own. "Doctor, thank you so much. I feel like myself again. I've started writing a new book. And my students seem pleased that I remember their names again!"

To be sure, not everyone who responds to T therapy has the same kind of dramatic response as Justin and Augustino. In fact, many men who begin treatment with testosterone never notice any benefits at all. This shouldn't be a surprise, because there is no treatment in the world that works for everyone and there can be any number of reasons why a man may feel drained or lacking in sexual interest. But the majority of men with low T do respond to treatment, often in ways that make their lives better.

One of the great hurdles in addressing the topic of low T is that we are talking about a loaded subject—testosterone. Everyone thinks they know something about testosterone, and most of that information has a negative taint. A research colleague laughed when I described the difficulties in having T therapy accepted on a wider basis. "The reason no one wants to take testosterone," he joked, "is because everyone considers it evil. Athletes like Barry Bonds use testosterone to cheat. And I bet my wife and her girl-friends would say they'd be happy if all testosterone were removed from the universe, based on the way they think it makes men behave."

Within medicine, there is also a bias against testosterone. Commonly heard criticisms are that the benefits are unproven, the diagnosis is complex, and the treatment increases the risk of pros-tate cancer. In my view, none of this is true—but it is perceived to be true, which may be an even greater hurdle for physicians.

Another argument is that the decline in testosterone is a nor-mal part of aging and thus should not be treated. This idea that we should not meddle with Mother Nature is hogwash. We med-dle with nature every day when it comes to our health. "Normal, natural aging" is associated with bad eyes, bad hearing, bad teeth, bad joints, bad blood vessels, bad hearts, and cancer. We treat all of these to improve the quality of life or to increase longevity. Should we withhold offering prescription glasses to older men and women because poor vision is common with advancing years and thus "normal"? It's a ridiculous notion. Low T is no different. Just because low T becomes more common as men age is no reason to deny treatment.

Not everyone agrees with my attitudes about testosterone. Indeed, some colleagues disagree quite strongly. As an example, an authoritative committee of the Endocrine Society issued a statement that comes down quite differently on several issues than I do. Yet when they published their views, many other experts protested vigorously. And on several issues I discuss in this book—such as the best blood test for testosterone or the best treatment for testosterone deficiency—expert committees have often deadlocked, unable to reach consensus.

In presenting my views, I want to make it clear that I am speaking for myself alone. In this book, I will do my best to describe differing opinions held by others and why I think that the evidence supports my position, not theirs. I will say up front that I believe the benefits of treating low T outweigh the risks for most men. I believe treatment can help men regain their ability to lead full, loving, satisfying lives. I believe that many doctors have not kept up with the latest research about both the benefits and the risks of T therapy and are therefore doing some patients a disservice by not treating low T. At the same time, I want to make it clear that I do not think that testosterone treatment should be given to men *unless* they have symptoms or signs of low T and have test results confirming they have low T.

Several years ago I wrote in *Sports Illustrated* that professional golfer Shaun Micheel should not be penalized for receiving treatment for low T. Shaun is not a patient of mine, but he and I had done a series of radio interviews on the topic of low T for Father's Day a few years ago. Shaun described feeling "foggy" as he stood over his putts and no longer having the motivation to practice on the driving range. His doctor diagnosed low T with a blood test, and when Shaun's testosterone had normalized with treatment, he had regained his focus, mental clarity, and motivation again. In response to criticism that Shaun was cheating by using testosterone, I explained that low T was a medical condition and that the goal of T therapy was not to enhance Shaun's performance but only to allow him to perform at the same level as he would have done without this hormone deficiency.

Not all of my colleagues agree with me. But those same colleagues would not have refrained from giving Shaun thyroid pills if he had thyroid deficiency. What is the difference? If a person's body does not make enough of a hormone, if the low levels of the hormone cause symptoms that disrupt a person's life, if treatment has been shown to improve those symptoms, and if the treatment does not produce risks that outweigh the benefits of improved symptoms, then why not give the treatment?

Professional sports organizations are entitled to make their own rules, but the point is the same whether one is a pro golfer or just a regular guy: treatment of low T can give a man the opportunity to reclaim his full potential and to live a satisfying and happy life.

The great news about low T is that attitudes are changing; there is an increasing awareness and willingness on the part of physicians to diagnose and treat low T. It seems that every month there is new research teaching us more and more about the effects of low T and the benefits of treatment. Much of this new work suggests that having normal levels of testosterone is beneficial for our health in general, with some studies even showing that men with normal testosterone levels live longer than men with untreated low levels of testosterone. And it has been especially gratifying to see the demise of the old fear that raising testosterone will increase the risk of prostate cancer, a topic that has been the focus of much of my research and scientific writing.

This book is for you if you feel you may have the symptoms of low T—low energy, chronic fatigue, low sex drive, poor quality erections, loss of muscle bulk and strength—or if you have already been diagnosed with low T and want to learn more about it. I have organized the book so that you can read it straight through, or you can read just selected chapters, depending on your interests. In Chapter 1, I share stories from my practice so that you can get a feel for the various ways that low T can impact a man and his life (personal information has been altered to preserve privacy). Chapter 2 is devoted to explaining what testosterone is and what it does. Readers may be surprised to learn the ways that testosterone influences boys and girls before and after puberty.

In Chapter 3, I describe the various symptoms caused by low T, and Chapter 4 addresses the various blood tests used to diagnose low T and how to interpret them properly. Chapter 5 reviews the benefits of T therapy in men, and Chapter 6 describes the different ways that low T can be treated, with pills, patches, gels, pellets, and injections.

Chapter 7 addresses the specific concern regarding testosterone and prostate cancer. For sixty-five years, it had been assumed that raising testosterone will increase the risk of prostate cancer, or would make an existing prostate cancer grow more rapidly. As I will explain later in the book, this idea was not unreasonable. However, it was allowed to stand unchallenged for fifty years and was not critically examined until quite recently. New information now strongly suggests that T therapy is quite safe for the prostate. In this chapter, I also describe my exciting journey researching this topic, with perhaps my greatest discovery occurring not in the laboratory, but in the basement of the Countway Medical Library at Harvard Medical School. With any treatment, it is important to learn about its risks, which are covered in Chapter 8.

Chapter 9 is special because it addresses for the first time the difficult situation of treating low T in prostate cancer survivors.

Until now, a prior history of prostate cancer was considered the single most important reason for *not* giving T therapy. This is a holdover from the old fear that higher testosterone will make hidden prostate cancer cells grow. Yet there are now very large numbers of men who have been cured of their prostate cancer, often in the prime of their lives, and who desire treatment for their symptoms from low T. In this chapter, I provide some guidance for these men. Although no large study of T therapy has yet been performed in men who have been treated for prostate cancer, there is new evidence that T therapy may actually be reasonably safe for some men after prostate cancer treatment. Finally, Chapter 10 provides a peek into the future of testosterone and T therapy and its potential to improve health and longevity.

Are you ready to see if testosterone therapy might change your life? Let's get started.

Chapter 1

Recognizing the Symptoms

This book is written to help men determine whether they have low testosterone and, if so, how best to obtain treatment. The first step, then, is to recognize the symptoms of low testosterone, or low T.

As many as 20 percent of men over fifty years of age may have low levels of testosterone in their bloodstream, but only a fraction of this number have symptoms. As more research is done and low T is better understood, it is possible, perhaps even likely, that we will come to treat asymptomatic men as well. There is growing evidence, for example, that low T is associated with an increased risk of diabetes, atherosclerosis (hardening of the arteries, which can lead to heart attacks or strokes), and weak bones, but as yet these observations are not reason enough to begin testosterone treatment. At this time, the primary reason to treat men with low T is to alleviate symptoms.

Testosterone has a wide variety of actions throughout the body, so it should be no surprise that there are multiple symptoms of low T. Some men may have just one symptom, while others may have a whole list of symptoms, all of which may be addressed by testosterone treatment.

As you read these stories, see if you recognize yourself in any of them. Remember that everyone is different and that the symptoms of low T can be different from one individual to another. If you have one or more of the symptoms described by men in these stories, then it may be worthwhile for you to have a blood test to determine whether you have low T.

Low Sex Drive

The hallmark symptom of low T is low libido, or low sex drive. The relationship between testosterone and sex drive has been known for a long time, so that even when people have no medical background at all, if someone says he has no interest in sex, his friends may joke that he has "low testosterone."

Jerry was a fifty-four-year-old patient with a remarkable story. His first wife had passed away ten years earlier from cancer, and he had raised his two children into adulthood on his own. While he was working and taking care of his children, he felt he didn't have time for a relationship. Now that his kids were on their own, he met and married a woman twelve years younger. "Clarice is great, and I'm very lucky to have such an attractive wife," he said. "But even though I know she's attractive, I just don't have the urge to do anything sexual with her." He paused for a moment. "Or with anyone, for that matter," he added.

Jerry described his situation further. "It's like a part of me is switched off. Once in a great while we have sex, maybe once every month or two. I can get hard, but I have to really concentrate to stay hard, and it's a struggle. My other doctor gave me some of those erection pills—they did help me stay hard but didn't change my interest."

"How long has it been since you had a strong interest in sex?" I asked.

"I couldn't really tell you, Doctor. My first wife and I had an active sex life until we had kids, and then it changed a bit, like it probably does for everyone. But then she got sick, and I never really paid too much attention to sex until I met Clarice years later."

I asked Jerry what he hoped to achieve by his consultation with me, and he responded, "I actually don't want anything for myself. But Clarice deserves more from me. She's a younger woman, she took a chance on a guy like me with two kids already, and she deserves to have sex on a regular basis. She likes it, and she tells me she feels closer to me after it happens." Jerry shifted in his chair. "I'll tell you a story. Last Valentine's Day we went with three other couples up to this nice inn in Vermont for the night. We all had a great dinner, and then everyone joked about heading up to their rooms to have sex. When we got up to the room, I climbed into bed, turned off the light, and went to sleep. It was embarrassing."

Jerry's past medical history gave no clues as to what may have been causing his difficulties. Some medicines can cause sexual problems, but the only prescription medicine he took was for high cholesterol—a medicine that doesn't usually cause sexual problems. Depression can cause lack of sexual desire or performance, but Jerry had no history of depression. When his blood tests came back, however, it showed that his testosterone levels were low.

I started Jerry on testosterone treatment with gel. At first, he noted no changes in his sexual desire, and blood tests showed that his T levels had increased only into the lower range of normal. I then increased the dose of gel, and his blood tests showed excellent levels of testosterone, in the midrange of normal. Jerry reported that he started waking up with erections in the morning. "It's like seeing an old friend again," he said with some pleasure. This was a positive sign.

"Give it a couple of months now," I advised.

Two months later, Jerry returned with Clarice by his side. They made an interesting couple, Jerry his usual disheveled self and Clarice a petite, pretty woman who was well put-together.

"How are things going?" I asked, after Clarice and I had introduced ourselves.

They both smiled. "Great!" Jerry exclaimed. "Clarice says I'm like a teenager the way I'm after her all the time." Jerry looked over at Clarice and they seemed to share a momentary private joke. "I don't think it's *that* extreme," he said, "but we're having sex on a regular basis now, at least once or twice a week. And I think about sex again, even when we're not doing anything. I'd forgotten what that was like, but I remember that I used to do that all the time, before my first wife got sick."

"Have you noticed any other changes in Jerry since he started treatment?" I asked Clarice.

"Definitely," she replied. "It's hard to know whether it's the testosterone itself, or just one good thing leading to another, but Jerry seems happier. He jokes around with me in ways he only rarely did before. He makes decisions more quickly. For example, when I used to ask him what movie he wanted to see, he would usually just turn it around and ask me what I wanted to see. But now he'll tell me what he's interested in. It's like Jerry has emerged from his shell."

Clarice's description of the changes in Jerry was typical of what I hear from the partners of men treated with testosterone. Many times, men come in for a specific symptom, such as low libido or erectile dysfunction, and they evaluate the response to treatment by focusing only on those original symptoms. But subtle changes in how a man acts or the energy he gives off in day-to-day interactions may be less visible to the person himself, but obvious to the people around him. Often, the man will deny noticing any other changes with treatment, while his partner will turn to me and say with conviction, "Oh yeah, he's different."

One other point to make about Jerry's case. Although there can be a number of reasons why T levels can be low in men, the most common by far is the gradual decline in testosterone that accompanies aging. This doesn't mean that Jerry was old—some men will have normal T levels into their eighties. But it is often difficult to pinpoint the moment when libido changes or disappears. Slow changes can be difficult to notice, especially when they happen over many years and when there are major stresses going on in life. In Jerry's case, there was a period of many years when he was coping with the grief of his first wife's death and the challenges of raising his children alone. At some point during that stressful period, Jerry's testosterone levels likely dropped into the low range, but he didn't notice it because of everything else going on in his life. This is true for many men.

Low Energy, or "The Couch Speaks to Me"

I still laugh when I think of Richard's story. Like most physicians, I have my patients fill out a form before I see them on which they list their medical information, such as current medications, allergies, and prior operations. Near the top of the form is a line that asks, "What is your reason for seeing the doctor?"

In response to this question, Richard had written: "The couch speaks to me." I wasn't sure what this meant. When I entered the exam room, there was Richard, a tall, lanky guy, forty-six years old, who greeted me with a big smile and a shock of red hair hanging over his forehead, which he swept away with a big, calloused hand.

"So," I asked, curious, "what do you mean, 'The couch speaks to me'?"

"Doctor," Richard began, "I've always been a busy guy. I hold two jobs, not because I need the money, but because I like being busy. And on nights and weekends, I'm always in my shop in the basement, working on projects. Ever since I was a kid, I've been 'Go, go, go.' But over the last couple of years, every time I walk across my living room, I hear the couch call out to me, saying," and here Richard cupped his hands to his mouth, as if calling someone far away, "'Come! Lie down! Take a nap!'"

Richard grinned at me, pleased with his performance, and I couldn't help but laugh out loud. He went on, "Doc, taking naps in the middle of the day just isn't me. I'm not depressed, my life is great otherwise, I don't have any major stresses in my life. I just feel like there is something different about my body and my brain, and I'm wondering if it's low testosterone."

Richard denied having any other symptoms of low T. His erections were fine, his libido was strong, his mood was good and upbeat. The only thing he complained about was that he just didn't have the same energy level and drive to be busy that had defined him his whole life.

Sure enough, Richard's T levels came back low. I started him on testosterone therapy and saw him back in follow-up a couple of months later.

"How are you?" I asked.

"Doc," he replied, "the couch doesn't speak to me anymore. I'm cured."

Richard's story highlights the impact of low T on what we call energy or motivation or fatigue. Energy may sound like the opposite of fatigue, and motivation can be synonymous for energy in some circumstances, but many men make distinctions between these words in using them to describe how they feel. Another overlapping word and feeling is having a sense of vitality, a feeling of being alive. The loss of these can be due to low T, and all may resolve with treatment.

The subtlety of these feelings makes them hard to study. And sometimes the response to treatment may be more obvious to those around him than to the man himself. Many times I've heard the man's partner tell me, "There's something different about him. He just seems so much more . . . alive."

Erectile Dysfunction

Samuel was a seventy-two-year-old, wiry man who saw me for erectile dysfunction. "I've been married for forty-four years to the same wonderful woman. Doc, she's as beautiful today as the day she became my bride. But for the last two years, I just can't get an erection that's firm enough to have sex anymore. My regular doctor gave me a prescription for all three of the erection pills out there, Cialis, Viagra, Levitra, you name it, and they all help a little bit, but not enough to make a difference."

I asked about his libido. "Oh, the desire is there, all right." He gave me a wink. "No problem in that department. And we've figured out other ways to stay physical, if you get my meaning, and I can still come. But I'm just never hard anymore. Used to be that I would wake up with a good erection from time to time or masturbate and get hard, but not anymore."

Samuel's normal sexual desire suggested that maybe low T was not the source of his erection difficulties, which we often call ED, for the technical term *erectile dysfunction*. Samuel had other reasons to have ED—hypertension and high cholesterol can both contribute to vascular disease, which in turn can cause ED. Samuel also took a number of prescription medications for those problems, which can sometimes contribute to ED. Given his age and medical conditions, it would have been reasonable to assume that Samuel's erection problem was due to blood vessel problems, specifically atherosclerosis. Tests performed in my office did indeed show some compromise of Samuel's blood vessels to the penis. In addition, blood tests showed low levels of testosterone.

When Samuel returned to discuss his test results, I explained to him that he had at least two possible reasons for his ED, one being poor blood vessels and the other being low T. Although normalizing Samuel's testosterone would be highly unlikely to improve his blocked arteries, it might still help his erections.

Samuel agreed and returned three months after beginning therapy. "Good job, Doc," he said when I entered the room. "The testosterone isn't a home run, but at least I get on base now," he joked. "What I've noticed since starting the testosterone is that I get aroused more quickly, and my penis gets harder than before. It's still not hard enough for me to have sex without any help. But the important thing is that the pills work now—just about every time. I can have sex again as long as I remember to take a pill."

As I mentioned at the beginning of the chapter, men may have one symptom of low T without having any of the others. This was true for Samuel. His libido, the hallmark symptom of low T, was unaffected by his low T levels, and he did not notice any change when his T levels were increased. Samuel's ED, though, had a component that was due to the low T. Men seem to have individual "thermostats" or thresholds, for each of the various symptoms of low T.

Recent studies in humans and animals show that there are receptors for testosterone in the corpora cavernosa of the penis, the chambers where erection takes place. These receptors send out chemical signals that are involved in the erection process. No wonder, then, that testosterone treatment has been shown to "rescue" erections in men with ED who have already had treatment with the erection-enhancing pills.

In one study of men who had failed full-dose treatment with sildenafil (Viagra), treatment of low T resulted in one-third of the men being able to have sex without any other medications at all, another third being able to have sex with testosterone therapy and the erection pills combined, and the last third were still unable to have sex. Testosterone can be an effective treatment for many men with erectile dysfunction.

Decreased Muscle Mass

Jack came to see me for a different reason. Now fifty-eight years old, he'd been an athlete his whole life, making it as a professional football player briefly in his twenties, then slimming down as a "fitness freak," in his words, for the rest of his life. He participated in marathons, cycling events, and whatever else he could find to test his body.

"I know what my body is capable of and how it responds to exercise," Jack told me. "For the last year or two, when I go to the gym after being away from it for a few months, I just can't build up the way I used to. Over the last eight weeks, I've been stuck with the same weight when I bench-press and can't move up. In the past, I would have been adding more weight every week or two."

"How would you like me to help you?" I asked.

"I'm not looking for miracles," Jack said, "and I'm not interested in being Superman. Or Schwarzenegger," he smiled wryly. "But it's important to me to be fit, stay fit. Right now, I'm feeling old, and I never felt that way before. If you can help me feel the way I think I should, that would be great. My primary care doctor tested my blood and told me my testosterone was in the low-normal range, but he wasn't sure what to do about it or whether it was causing my symptoms because I don't have any sexual problems at all. So he suggested I talk to you about it."

I ran through the various symptoms of low T, and indeed, Jack had none of them other than the feeling that he wasn't as vigorous as he once was and that his muscular response to exercise wasn't as good as it had been in the past. One other symptom he noted was that it took longer for his body to recharge after a heavy workout. When I looked at Jack's previous lab results, his total testosterone, the test used by most physicians, was just within the normal range suggested by the laboratory, but it was actually indicative of low T.

Jack started treatment with testosterone. He didn't like the gels, because he worked out so frequently that he was afraid he would sweat it off, so he underwent injections in my office every two weeks. Later he learned how to give himself injections in the thigh. I monitored his levels closely because the goal was to get him back into the normal range for men, not to get his levels up into the stratosphere, like bodybuilders and athletes using steroids for performance enhancement.

Jack was gratified with the results. "I'm OK again," he volunteered. "I can't do what I did when I was twenty-five years old, but then, I'm not twenty-five anymore. I've been moving up on my weights in the gym, and my muscles recover more quickly from the big workouts. The big thing is, I don't feel like an old man anymore."

When It's Not Low Testosterone

As can be seen from the stories of these men, testosterone treatment in men with low T can produce a fairly wide number of beneficial results. Let's be clear, though, that testosterone is not the solution to every symptom, nor does it work in everyone. After all, even men with completely normal levels of testosterone can have ED, low sex drive, or poor energy. Sometimes the cause of a man's symptoms is just life—stress, medical conditions, relationship issues, trouble at work.

Two of the common factors that may cause symptoms suggestive of low T are depression and medications. Alphonse's story underscores this nicely. Alphonse was a forty-four-year-old construction worker who came in with his wife, Sherry. When I asked Alphonse how I could help him, he turned to Sherry. "Why don't you tell him?" he suggested.

"Al was diagnosed with diabetes three years ago, and then he became depressed. He's better now, but we have two problems. One is that he has almost no interest in sex. We have sex every three months or so. The other is that we'd like to have a baby. I've been off the pill for four years, and we don't use anything else for birth control. But if we don't have sex, it's obviously hard for me to get pregnant."

Sherry continued, "We've been through a lot together. When we first started talking about having a child together . . ." She paused and corrected herself. "When *I* first started talking about having a baby, Al didn't say no, but he didn't say yes. He seemed to be struggling with the idea, and I think part of what happened is that he didn't want to have sex with me because he wasn't ready to be a father. We've talked about it more over the last year or two, and now I think we're both ready. At least, Al seems ready. But we still almost never have sex."

Alphonse sat quietly, adding nothing to the story, but not appearing to disagree with Sherry at all. In fact, he seemed quite satisfied with her version of his feelings. Despite his few comments, Al and Sherry gave off a warm impression of a solid couple. When Sherry left the room so that I could examine Alphonse alone, I asked him how he felt about trying to become a father.

"Sherry got it right," he said. "I really didn't want to be a father when she first brought it up. But now I do. I look forward to it, actually. But I just don't have the feeling for sex anymore. It's not about Sherry, either. If Angelina Jolie came into my bed naked, I wouldn't get excited. It's like some switch inside me has been turned off."

It turned out that Alphonse's medications included two antidepressants, one of which was in the class called selective serotonin reuptake inhibitors. An unfortunate side effect of this type of medication is that it lowers sex drive in many men and can also cause difficulty achieving orgasm. Depression can also cause diminished or even absent libido, but Alphonse and Sherry both seemed satisfied that his depression had lifted.

A semen analysis for Alphonse was normal, so there was no concern about his fertility. However, blood tests revealed that he had low T. Because the likely cause of Alphonse's low sex drive was his antidepressant medication, it was uncertain whether raising his testosterone level would have any effect on his libido. Nevertheless, Alphonse and Sherry thought it was worth a try, particularly because Alphonse was understandably reluctant to change the medication regimen that had cured his depression. I prescribed a pill that would hopefully increase Alphonse's own production of testosterone without lowering his sperm counts, which can be a side effect of testosterone gels and injections.

Unfortunately, despite successfully raising Alphonse's testosterone levels well into the normal range, the medication had no effect on his libido. We discontinued the medication. I advised Alphonse that when he was ready, he could speak with his psychiatrist about changing his medications to another type that would not have sexual side effects and that there was a good chance his libido would then return. I had nothing else to offer him.

Eighteen months later, my secretary told me I had an unscheduled visitor. Waiting for me in one of the exam rooms were Alphonse and Sherry, and in Alphonse's arms lay a tiny, new baby girl. "We just wanted you to meet Frances," he said, beaming. Alphonse had changed his medications under his psychiatrist's supervision, and his libido had returned almost immediately. "Within a short while after changing medications, that switch I had mentioned got flipped back on," he explained.

Testosterone treatment is not a panacea. In many cases, low sex drive, poor erections, or increased fatigue may have nothing to do with testosterone, which is why it's important to understand how testosterone works and when it might help. The first step is to see an interested physician and to have a blood test to determine whether your testosterone levels are low. When characteristic symptoms are confirmed by low levels of testosterone, it is time to consider a trial of testosterone therapy. For many men—and for those who love them—testosterone treatment can make an enormous difference in their lives.

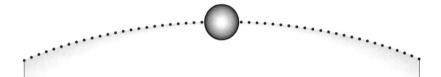

Questions and Answers

Q. *Is it true that if a person has a normal sex drive, then he must have normal T levels?*

A. No. Low T can show up in a variety of ways, and the sex drive (also known as libido) for some men seems to be unaffected by low T, even though they may have other symptoms that respond to testosterone therapy. In addition, the decline in T levels usually occurs over many years, and it can be exceedingly difficult to compare the intensity of one's sex drive today to that of a few years ago. Some men who claim to have a normal sex drive will come back to the office after beginning T therapy and say, "Wow, I'd forgotten what it was like to have a sex drive like this!"

Q. *What is the difference between symptoms of low T and signs of low T?*

A. Symptoms are things we experience, and signs are things that can be measured by another person or a machine. The most common symptoms of low T are diminished libido, erectile dysfunction, low energy, increased fatigue, reduced strength, depressed mood, and decreased sense of vitality. The most common signs of low T are reduced bone density and a low red blood cell concentration in the blood, which is called anemia.

Q. *Aren't the symptoms of low T similar to the symptoms of depression?*

A. Yes, there is considerable overlap. The situation is confounded further by the fact that many men with depression have low T and that testosterone therapy often improves mood. Usually, the mood symptoms of most men with low T are fairly mild. Some men will say they feel gray, blah, or washed out.

However, if someone has symptoms of major depression—suicidal thoughts or feelings of being hopeless, helpless, and worthless—then it is critical that the individual seek professional psychiatric help immediately. Testosterone therapy has no role in the treatment of individuals with serious depression.

Q. *Are there other causes of low libido?*

A. The three primary causes of low libido are low T, depression, and medications. Of the medications, the ones that most commonly cause low libido are the frequently prescribed antidepressants known as selective serotonin reuptake inhibitors (SSRIs). A few of the most commonly prescribed SSRIs are Prozac, Zoloft, and Paxil.

Q. *If someone does have strong sexual desire, but it occurs infrequently, would that also be considered low libido?*

A. Low libido can mean reduced overall desire, infrequent desire, or absent desire. Low T can cause all of these.

Q. *Is it true that men who develop low T, such as after an injury to the testicles, will have high-pitched voices?*

A. No. The pitch of the voice is determined mainly by the size of the larynx, or voicebox. This enlarges at puberty under the influence of testosterone and often becomes visible in the neck as the Adam's apple. However, losing testosterone as an adult does not result in shrinkage of the larynx, and thus there is no change in the pitch of a man's voice with low T.

Q. *Does low T lead to homosexuality?*

A. No.

Q. *Does high T lead to homosexuality?*

A. No.

Q. *Don't many things cause low energy, other than low T?*

A. Yes. The experience of feeling blah or having low energy does not necessarily mean that a man has low T. Unless there is an obvious explanation for the lack of energy, the presence of these symptoms does mean that it is worthwhile to check for the presence of low T.

Q. *My penis feels dead or numb. Can this be related to low T?*

A. The first time a patient told me his penis was numb, I was worried he had a neurologic disorder and pinched it hard, expecting him to not feel much. When he jumped halfway into the next room, I learned that the feeling of penile numbness some men experience with low T is not a nerve disorder but is the absence of that special electricity or responsiveness men feel when they see or feel something sexually arousing. Normal sensation for touch or pain is not affected. This feeling usually returns when testosterone is normalized. And I've learned to be more gentle.

Chapter 2

Testosterone and Your Health

Understanding Testosterone

Before determining whether someone has low testosterone, it is important to understand what testosterone is, how it works, and how it is regulated by the body. From time immemorial, physicians as well as those who own farm animals have been aware of a critical relationship between the testicles and male behavior. It was only in the twentieth century, however, that testosterone was determined to be the key substance made by the testicles that conferred the characteristics of manhood.

The History of Testosterone

The history of testosterone is a colorful one, as might be expected from its association with masculinity and the testicles. For several thousand years, farmers have found that castrating domesticated animals made them infertile and more docile as well as greatly reducing their sexual activity. They did not know, however, that they were reducing a specific substance, because testosterone was not identified until the 1930s. All that was known was that removing the testicles resulted in reliable changes in animal behaviors that we associate with maleness.

One of the first true research experiments in this area was reported in 1849 by Arnold Berthold, who showed that the coxcomb of the rooster shrunk in size when the animal was castrated, but not when the nerves of the testicle were severed. This suggested that whatever it was that the testicles were producing to create the masculinizing effect had nothing to do with nerves and was thus more likely a substance that was secreted into the bloodstream.

On June 1, 1889, at a French scientific meeting, Charles-Édouard Brown-Séquard piqued the interest of the medical world as well as the public when he reported that he had injected into himself an extract made from the testicles of dogs and guinea pigs. He claimed that this extract, soon known as The Elixir of Life, increased his strength, appetite, and mental acuity, but he provided no data of any sort to support this claim. Nevertheless, a new field called organotherapy was born, in which tissues and organs from animals or humans were injected into people with the anticipated effect of creating qualities in the recipient that matched the alleged qualities of the original tissues. For testicular extracts, this was assumed to be the qualities one associates with virility and youthfulness. Organotherapy became widely popular and, in some form, was used to treat a wide variety of additional ailments, including epilepsy, diabetes, and tuberculosis. It was estimated that by the end of that same year, twelve thousand individuals had been treated with some form of this therapy.

In 1920, a Viennese physiologist named Eugene Steinach had a somewhat similar idea. His goal was to increase the secretion of the unknown testicular substance to alleviate symptoms in "middle-aged, listless individuals." Steinach developed a procedure in which he tied off one of the vasa deferentia, the tubes that carry the sperm and related fluid from the testicle. This was essentially half of what we call today a vasectomy. Steinach believed that by tying off the tube carrying sperm, the testicle would have no choice but to secrete more of its essence into the bloodstream. This procedure attained modest popularity for the next two decades, and it has been reported that individuals as noteworthy as Sigmund Freud and W. B. Yeats underwent the Steinach procedure.

Efforts to produce rejuvenation using testicular tissues had some proponents as late as the 1960s, when a surgeon named Paul Niehan proposed the injection of trillions of testicular cells into the body. His theory was that the injection of these "young" or "embryonic" cells would offer the recipient's body the same youthfulness and vitality of those cells themselves. It has been reported that Pope Pius XII and Aristotle Onassis underwent this treatment.

We know today that none of these treatments had any chance of working, primarily because the immune system recognizes and eliminates any cells it considers foreign, whether from other humans or from other animal species. This is why transplantation of organs such as kidneys and livers was so difficult to achieve until the development of immunosuppressant medications that allowed foreign cells and tissues to grow in the recipient without rejection.

But we should not disparage the inventors of those early techniques, nor the individuals who allowed themselves to be treated. After all, the substance that created the masculine effect was clearly produced in the testicles, though no one knew how it worked or what it was, so efforts to increase this substance may have seemed reasonable at the time. And clearly, there was a palpable desire of men in their middle years to regain some of the qualities of their youth, such as greater sex drive, sexual ability, strength, motivation, and a sense of vitality. There is no reason to believe that the symptoms of testosterone deficiency were any less prevalent in the 1800s and early 1900s than they are now.

With the discovery of the actual testosterone molecule in the early 1930s came a new approach to this issue. Not only was testosterone identified, but soon there were tests to measure it. Perhaps of greatest eventual significance, it was only a few years later, in 1935, that testosterone would be synthesized and made available as an injectable medication. The original scientists who learned to synthesize testosterone, a Swiss chemist named Leopold Ružička and a German named Adolf Butenandt, were awarded the Nobel Prize in Chemistry for this work in 1939.

What Is Testosterone?

We've come a long way from the unscientific experiments of the previous two centuries. Testosterone has been extensively studied; a computer search of scientific articles on testosterone yields over five thousand papers in the last five years alone.

Because testosterone has so many different effects on the body, testosterone research involves a body of scientific literature that is astoundingly diverse. Today, we know that testosterone has important actions on embryological development, brain function, sexuality, muscle, bone, red blood cells, and mood, to name some of the best-studied areas. Later, I will describe the important points about testosterone's actions in these different areas, but first I need to explain the different forms that it takes in the body.

The Hormone Testosterone

Testosterone is a hormone, which simply means it is a chemical produced by one part of the body that acts somewhere else in the body, usually transported via the bloodstream. Another example of a hormone is insulin, which is made by the pancreas and circulates throughout the body, controlling the way that cells use the sugar glucose.

Testosterone is produced by the Leydig cells of the testicles, and most of it is secreted into the bloodstream, traveling to locations as distant as the brain. Some testosterone remains in the testicles themselves, helping to produce an environment conducive to the production of mature sperm. It should be no surprise, then, that some men with low numbers of sperm also have low T concentrations.

Estradiol

Once testosterone reaches its distant target organs, it may either function directly as testosterone itself or be altered by enzymes in those cells to become different hormones with different characteristics and functions. For example, an enzyme called aromatase takes testosterone and converts it into estradiol, which is a primary type of estrogen. A good deal of aromatase is found in fatty tissue. This explains in part why overweight men are often found to have enlargement of their breasts, a condition called gynecomastia, because the conversion of testosterone to estradiol stimulates breast tissue growth.

DHT

Testosterone is also converted by some tissues to the molecule dihydrotestosterone (DHT). DHT has three actions of great importance for men—the first is that it is necessary for proper development of the male genitalia during fetal life. The second is that it is primarily responsible for prostate growth, and the third is that its actions on the scalp are responsible for hair loss, or male pattern baldness. No DHT, no balding. Thankfully, higher testosterone levels do not appear to lead to increased hair loss.

The action of DHT on the prostate may have less cosmetic impact, but has greater medical importance. Both testosterone and DHT have the capability of stimulating prostate growth, but

DHT is ten times more potent within the prostate. When physicians refer to the action of testosterone on the prostate, they are usually being imprecise using testosterone as shorthand for its actual effects via conversion to DHT.

This relationship between testosterone and DHT has allowed for the production of medications that can specifically target the enzyme responsible for the conversion between these two hormones. Because prostates shrink when deprived of DHT, medications that block the conversion of testosterone to DHT have been effective in reducing prostate size and improving the urination symptoms that often accompany enlarged prostates. The first medication of this type, finasteride (trade name: Proscar), was heavily prescribed for men when it first came out. A newer version of this type of medication, called dutasteride (trade name: Avodart), is even more specific in its actions on prostatic DHT. On average, these medications reduce prostate size by roughly one-third and can greatly reduce urinary frequency and urgency in many men.

Because DHT is also responsible for hair loss, some bright soul figured out that finasteride might also be helpful in this area. A lower dosage of finasteride was relabeled as Propecia and remains a common treatment for male pattern baldness. It appears that reducing DHT in this way may be most effective in reducing further loss of hair rather than promoting new hair growth, although individual results vary considerably.

Anabolic Steroids

Testosterone is an anabolic steroid. Although news stories and magazines have given the word *steroid* a dangerous, dark connotation, as if it were the equivalent of heroin, the truth is that every one of us is filled with steroids and we would be unable to live without them. The term *steroid* refers to molecules that have a particular chemical structure, or backbone, consisting of four carbon rings with various other atoms attached to them to give them their distinctive names and actions within the body. Anabolic steroids are chemicals that cause anabolism, an overall increase in protein production and storage, primarily seen as an increase in muscle and bone. The opposite of anabolism is catabolism, which occurs during starvation, for example, when the body starts breaking down protein in muscles to provide nutrients for the rest of the body.

Many of the important molecules in the body are steroids, especially those involved in sexual and reproductive actions for men and women. Other steroids come from the adrenal glands and include cortisol, which is a key molecule that helps regulate our immune system and response to stress. A surprise for most people is that the key building block for all of these molecules is cholesterol, which is also a steroid. Everyone knows that too much cholesterol is not good for one's health, but without any cholesterol we would be in deep trouble, because we would then have difficulty making any of the other steroids so necessary for our bodies.

Anabolic steroids build up muscle bulk and strength and come in a variety of forms. All of them are based on testosterone; indeed, testosterone is the original anabolic steroid. However, the illicit "designer drug" industry has come up with agents that are so potent that testosterone itself is only used infrequently by athletes and bodybuilders seeking to enhance their performance. These anabolic steroids are used at doses equivalent to more than twenty times normal testosterone levels.

The old saying that "a little knowledge can be a dangerous thing" applies when discussing testosterone therapy in the office. Germain was a remarkably healthy sixty-one-year-old bricklayer who had always prided himself on his strength, but he found he could now carry only lighter loads at work. He seemed relieved when I explained that his test results showed low T, which could certainly have contributed to his change in strength. And he seemed eager to begin treatment. But then he stopped himself and asked suspiciously, "Doctor, this medicine you're talking about for me—it's not a steroid, is it? 'Cause I don't want to be taking any steroids."

Germain emphasized the word *steroid* when he spoke, nearly spitting it out as if it were something dangerous and disgusting. Despite discussing with Germain the fact that his body already had large amounts of steroids circulating in his bloodstream and that the goal of treatment was only to restore his testosterone to the levels he had ten to fifteen years ago, Germain absolutely refused T therapy. Interestingly, he felt fine about treatment with clomiphene citrate (trade name: Clomid), a medication that is not itself a steroid but instead spurs the body to increase its own testosterone production.

In a follow-up three months later, Germain seemed pleased with his results. "Feel my arms," he directed me with a smile as he flexed his muscles. "It's not what it used to be, but not too bad for an old man." Germain had regained his old form and strength from a return to normal levels of the anabolic steroid testosterone.

Testosterone Regulation

As I mentioned earlier, testosterone is produced by the Leydig cells in the testicles. However, the testicle has the capacity to produce varying amounts of testosterone, and the signal controlling the production of testosterone comes from a hormone made in the pituitary gland (a part of the brain behind the sinuses) called luteinizing hormone (LH). In turn, LH secretion is controlled by another hormone, called luteinizing hormone–releasing hormone (LHRH), that comes from another part of the brain nearby called the hypothalamus.

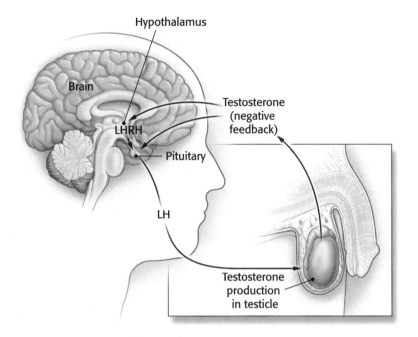

Control of Testosterone Production

The testicles produce testosterone and secrete it into the bloodstream so that it can travel throughout the body to exert its effects. Testosterone is a hormone produced under the control of luteinizing hormone (LH), which is produced by the pituitary gland in the brain. Higher levels of LH lead to greater testosterone production. LH release into the bloodstream is in turn stimulated by another hormone called LHRH that is produced by another area of the brain, the hypothalamus. Adequate or high testosterone levels are sensed by the hypothalamus and pituitary, resulting in lower levels of LHRH and LH in a process called negative feedback.

This three-part system is often referred to as the HPG axis, referring to the hypothalamus, pituitary, and gonad (testicle). There is one more important feature of the HPG system, which is a negative feedback system. Basically, both the hypothalamus and the pituitary recognize when testosterone levels are high, which causes lower secretion of LHRH and LH; the T levels themselves become reduced when this happens.

Understanding how the HPG system works is important. If a man has low T levels accompanied also by low LH levels, this means there is a problem with the hypothalamus or pituitary and the testicles are not receiving a strong enough signal to produce adequate amounts of testosterone. On the other hand, if T levels are low and LH levels are high, this means the problem is within the testicles, because the signal to produce testosterone is abundant. Most commonly when testosterone is low, particularly when it is due to aging, LH is actually within the normal range.

An important thing to keep in mind about testosterone treatment is how it relates to male fertility. One of the effects of giving testosterone as a treatment is that the hypothalamus and pituitary sense substantial levels of testosterone in the blood and therefore reduce the secretion of LH. This has the effect of turning off testosterone production within the testicle itself; the testicles, in a sense, go to sleep. They may become smaller and softer, and sperm production will be greatly reduced, sometimes to nothing, because of the lack of local production of testosterone. So, although men with infertility problems often have low T, treating them with additional testosterone produces the opposite effect from what is desired.

How Testosterone Affects the Brain and Body

The wide range of testosterone effects make it one of the body's most fascinating chemicals and also underscores why having normal levels of testosterone may be so desirable.

Testosterone and Development

Some years ago when I was waiting to pick up my older daughter, who was then four years old, from preschool, I began a conversation with Claudia, an architect and the mother of a four-year-old boy in the class. Several of the boys were running around the room, yelling war cries and causing general mayhem, while in front of us was a group of girls playing quietly in the make-believe kitchen. We

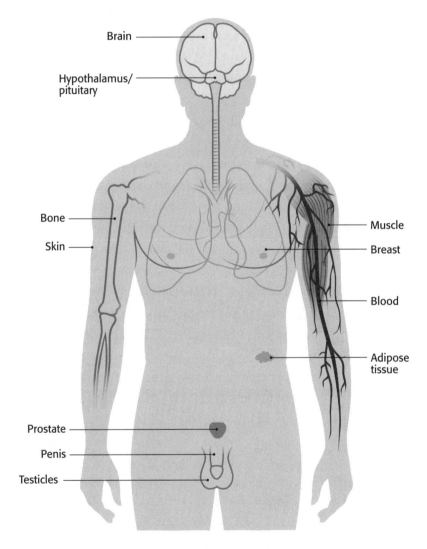

Effects of Testosterone on the Body

Testosterone acts on many organs and tissues in the body. It is critical for the production of sperm in the testicles, allows normal erections to take place, and has important actions on bone, muscle, the prostate, and the brain.

both laughed about the obvious behavioral differences between the boys and girls.

"When Jacob was born," Claudia remarked, "I believed strongly that environment had the greatest influence in how children grow up. So, to keep Jacob from becoming too aggressive or violent, my husband and I decided that no toy guns would ever enter our house. Not even water pistols. But I changed my ideas when one day Jacob pretended to shoot the dog and the cat with a gun he had fashioned from French toast. It was obvious to me that biology plays a huge role in how we act." We watched the boys bump into each other, fall to the ground, and laugh. She continued, "I guess you can't fight the effects of testosterone."

This notion that testosterone is what makes boys behave like boys—and its absence is what allows girls to be dainty girls—is quite prevalent. Claudia, a highly educated woman, would have been shocked to learn that there was no difference in testosterone levels between Jacob, running around like a tiny gladiator, and the little girls having a polite tea party. Testosterone can't explain all the differences in behavior because, prior to puberty, boys and girls have the same, very low concentrations of testosterone in their blood. At puberty, testosterone rises dramatically in boys. It also rises in girls at puberty, but to a much lesser extent.

Yet Claudia was not completely mistaken that testosterone had something to do with the boys' behavior. One of the ways that testosterone is important as a developmental hormone is that during fetal development and also shortly after birth, there is a transient surge in testosterone in boys, but not girls. Among other effects, it is believed that this rise in testosterone, even before birth, imprints the brain to be "boylike." If it doesn't happen, development happens as if the brain were female. Even though Jacob had nearly undetectable T levels, his behavior in all likelihood was indeed related to testosterone.

In addition to imprinting the brain, testosterone is also important for the development of the male genitalia. Testosterone is believed to play a critical role in development of the tubes and glands that allow sperm to travel from the testicles to the prostate. These structures include the epididymis, the vas deferens (the tube that is cut and tied off when a man has a vasectomy), and the seminal vesicles (the structure that makes most of the semen). In the fetus, these three structures together are called the Wolffian duct system, and their proper development requires an early dose of testosterone at the right time.

However, the actions of DHT, the molecule that is a slightly altered form of testosterone, is even more important for a baby to come out looking like a boy. In the developing fetus, DHT is responsible for the labia to fuse together in the midline to form a scrotum and for creation of the urine passageway, called the urethra, to form on the underside of the penis. Without DHT, boys would have the appearance of girls.

A genetic defect can block the conversion of testosterone to DHT. In fact, there is one well-studied tribe in the Dominican Republic in which a number of males have this defect, due to a high rate of inbreeding. These boys are born with their external genitalia looking like a female's—with labia instead of a scrotum and with a small penis that looks a great deal like a prominent clitoris. These babies are believed to be girls when born and are raised with the other girls. It is only when puberty occurs and their testosterone levels go through the roof that it becomes obvious these little "girls" are really boys. Although it is too late by this time to form a normal-looking scrotum, these individuals gain the appearance of adolescent boys and develop facial hair and deeper voices as well as masculine muscle development and definition.

A fascinating part of the story is that because this tribe has a history of girls occasionally becoming boys during puberty, there appears to be little shock amongst the members of this particular tribe when it occurs. These individuals are accepted as boys even though they had spent the first ten or twelve years of their lives as girls. Imagine how much more complicated this would be in our culture!

Testosterone and the Brain

Studies in humans and other animals have clearly demonstrated that testosterone has receptors in the brain and that it affects how we think and act. Some of these effects are related to sexual behavior, by acting on those parts of the brain that organize and control our sexual thoughts and behaviors. In humans, there is growing evidence that testosterone plays a role in some kinds of thinking abilities, as well as in mood, which is also a brain function.

When I was an undergraduate at Harvard working in a laboratory, I worked on a research project in which we examined the effects of testosterone on the sexual behavior of lizards. Normally, male lizards placed in a cage with a female go through a series of behaviors in which they demonstrate their sexual interest and then mate. The first step is extending the brightly colored skin under their neck, called a dewlap. Then the male does a set of rapid, repeating push-ups. In response, the female will do a simple, less showy push-up of her own. The male approaches closer, repeats his behavior, and finally pounces on the female, grabs her by the neck with his mouth, and they mate.

However, if the male has been castrated (testicles removed) and then placed with a female, he acts as if he doesn't even know she is in the same cage. He doesn't extend his dewlap, won't do his push-ups, and definitely won't try to mate. But when tiny amounts of testosterone were placed in specific areas of the brain that control sexual behavior, the male lizards resumed all their normal sexual behaviors, even though blood levels of testosterone were undetectable. This experiment in lizards, and similar ones in rats and other species, show unequivocally that testosterone has direct actions on the brain.

By the way, for those concerned about those poor female lizards subjected to sexually aggressive males—not to worry. The female only allows herself to be caught if she is sexually receptive. If the female has had her ovaries removed, resulting in low hormone levels of her own, she becomes unreceptive, and the males can chase her all day long without success. There is little doubt that hormones are critical for women as well as men when it comes to sex.

Testosterone and Sex

Testosterone plays a critical role in male sexuality. Not only does it work on the sexual centers in the brain, as described earlier, but it also works on the male sexual organs—penis, testicles, prostate, and seminal vesicles.

One of the best known effects of low T is erectile dysfunction. It has been known for many centuries that castrated men, meaning men whose testicles have been removed, lose the ability to have erections. Until the last fifteen years or so, this was believed to be almost exclusively due to the loss of sex drive because of testosterone's actions on the brain. But animal research has shown that there are receptors for testosterone in the corpora cavernosa, the two chambers of the penis where erections take place.

It was soon found that testosterone governed some of the chemical signals that controlled blood flow during the erection process and that animals with low T made less of the signal. A set of experiments showing conclusively that testosterone is critical for erections were made by my colleague, Abdul Traish, Professor of Biochemistry and Urology at Boston University.

Professor Traish has set up a model for monitoring erections in the rabbit. Under anesthesia, the nerves in the pelvis that control erection can be electrically stimulated to create an erection, and pressure within the penis can then be monitored. Under normal conditions, a full erection is achieved within seconds of nerve stimulation. When the animals have been castrated, however, nerve stimulation results in almost no rigidity at all. Restoring testosterone with injections causes the erectile response to be completely restored.

Something very interesting was noted when the penis tissue of these castrated animals was examined microscopically. Normally, the corpora cavernosa are filled almost exclusively with smooth muscle cells and blood vessels. Remarkably, in the castrated animals, a collection of another type of cells was found—fat cells. Even more interesting, the location of these fatty deposits was just underneath the sheath that surrounds the corpora cavernosa, where the mechanism to trap blood in the erectile chambers normally occurs via action of the smooth muscle cells. Replacing the smooth muscle cells with fat cells almost certainly contributes to the lack of normal erection with direct stimulation, because the trapping of blood will be ineffective.

In humans, Dr. Aksam Yassin of Germany has shown with X-rays that some men with low T who have erectile dysfunction (ED) due to poor trapping of blood within the corpora cavernosa respond to testosterone therapy by improving the effectiveness of blood trapping. T therapy allows the chambers to become "watertight" again, leading to improved erections. This appears to be the human equivalent to the effects shown by Professor Traish in animals.

Thus testosterone is critical not only for how the brain responds to sexual thoughts and stimulation, but also for the proper function of the penis, by affecting its ability to get hard, to release the necessary chemical signals, and to maintain the proper types of cells that are essential for good erectile function.

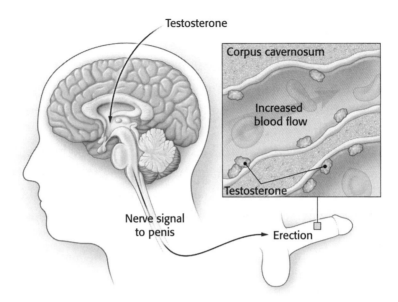

Effect of Testosterone on Erections

Testosterone has two important actions to help with erections. One is its actions on the sexual centers within the brain to convert arousing thoughts and sensations into nerve signals that are sent down the spinal cord to the blood vessels of the penis. The second is its direct actions within the penis to produce chemicals that contribute to creating an erection.

Testosterone and Muscles

The effect of testosterone on muscles explains in part why the average man is stronger, runs faster, and has greater muscle definition than the average woman. The reason that athletes and bodybuilders at the top of their careers put their reputations at risk by taking anabolic steroids is that these agents actually work. Muscle cells respond to higher testosterone levels by increasing in size and strength. And although it was believed for many years that no new muscle cells could be created in a mature individual, there is now evidence that, under the influence of testosterone, new cells are indeed created.

There is, however, an important distinction between the abuse of steroids and the medical use of testosterone to treat men with testosterone deficiency. The goal of T treatment is physiologic replacement, the restoration of testosterone to normal levels in someone who has too little. In contrast, athletes and bodybuilders take steroids at levels that are many times higher than the highest T levels ever found in normal men. They combine multiple chemicals at a time, usually for relatively short bursts of time, followed by periods of "recovery."

This difference between normal T replacement and steroid abuse for performance enhancement may seem subtle, but it is important. Athletes and bodybuilders use testosterone-like compounds at levels far above normal levels to achieve results that are otherwise impossible. Men with low T receive treatment to restore T levels into the normal range and to reach the potential they would have had without a hormone deficiency.

Testosterone and Fat

One of the unsung features of testosterone is that it acts on the fat cells in the body and tends to reduce body fat. Men with low T often have extra weight in the midsection, called truncal obesity, and may also have fatty breast tissue. Testosterone treatment often reduces the amount of fat in these areas, so that the breast tissue may shrink and waist size may decrease as well.

Of course, testosterone is not a cure for obesity, by any stretch of the imagination. No matter what level of testosterone a man has, if he takes in more calories than he uses up, the extra calories will be converted to fat. But in study after study, hypogonadal (the technical term for low T) men who were treated with testosterone had an increase in lean body mass (muscle) and a decrease in fat mass.

The mechanism by which testosterone has this effect on fatty tissues is not completely understood, although it is an area of active research. So far, what is clear is that testosterone alters the way fat cells, called adipocytes, handle the body's fuels circulating in the bloodstream.

Testosterone and Bones

I was pleasantly surprised when my younger daughter, at twelve years old, informed me that she needed to drink her milk and get calcium so she wouldn't develop osteoporosis. I was impressed with the way the information about bone density had reached down into the preteen years. Yet although this knowledge about women and osteoporosis is common, most health-conscious people are unaware that men can also be at risk for osteoporosis. Especially men with low T.

It turns out that testosterone is important for bone density. The reason that women are at risk for osteoporosis is that their estrogen levels decrease after menopause, and estrogen is one of the key chemicals responsible for bone growth and maintenance. Bone is constantly being broken down and built up, and estrogen helps with this balance. The effect of testosterone on bone has been shown to be partly through conversion to estradiol, a form of estrogen, and partly as a direct effect.

Not only does testosterone treatment increase bone density at the hip and spine in most studies, but men who have had their testosterone lowered, usually as part of a treatment for prostate cancer, have been shown to be at increased risk for osteoporosis and for fractures. Thus most men who will be on T-lowering agents for some time will also be started on medicines that help stabilize bone density.

Current recommendations are to obtain a bone density test in men with testosterone deficiency. If the numbers are low, the test should be repeated every year to monitor changes. If the numbers are normal, the test should be repeated every two years.

Putting It All Together

You can see why having normal testosterone levels can be so important. Yet when describing some of testosterone's functions separately, it is too easy to lose sight of its overall effect on the body.

What really struck me when I started doing this work was how much men improved when they responded to testosterone treatment. Although the primary reason men were referred to me was for some form of sexual dysfunction, usually ED or low libido, one of the unexpected rewards was hearing so many of my patients tell me how much better they felt in ways that had nothing to do directly with the symptoms I was treating. The majority described improvement in their sexual function, but many also described other gains: their moods were better, their partners found them less irritable, their workouts at the gym were improved. Often, they felt more motivated, brighter, and energetic.

What I realized then, and have learned to appreciate since, is the many ways that having normal testosterone levels can help a man feel his best. Although I warn my patients who are about to begin T treatment that they may not feel a dramatic, sudden change, like a light switch being turned on, the general improvement is often obvious to those around them. As one chronically grumpy patient described it recently, "I still have my daily ups and downs. But my wife, my primary care doctor, and my cardiologist all say I seem happier since I started testosterone. Something good must definitely be happening if all of them agree."

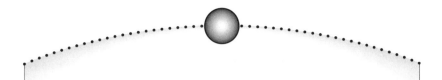

Questions and Answers

Q. *Is testosterone the reason men are more violent than women?*

A. No. There is no compelling evidence that testosterone is related to violence.

Q. *Is it true that criminals have higher T levels than noncriminals?*

A. No.

Q. *Does testosterone have any important functions in women?*

A. Early evidence suggests that testosterone is important for full sexual function in women as well as in men, particularly for libido.

Q. *Is T therapy an effective treatment for male infertility?*

A. No. In fact, testosterone has been investigated as a possible male contraceptive because it tends to lower sperm values to zero, or close to zero. Adding testosterone to men activates the negative feedback system, which, in turn, results in reduced sperm production. However, alternative treatments are available to stimulate higher testosterone production in the testicles, which may lead to greater sperm production in some men.

Q. *What happens if the developing male fetus is never exposed to testosterone?*

A. Remarkably, a genetically male boy will be born looking like a perfect little girl if for some reason his body did not make testosterone during critical steps in fetal life. Some individuals have a condition called testosterone insensitivity: these babies are born with testicles inside the body, where they make normal amounts of testosterone, but a genetic defect prevents their bodies from recognizing the hormone. They develop as girls, and the diagnosis is usually made when these individuals fail to get their first menstrual cycle despite an advanced age.

Q. *Does testosterone have anything to do with erections other than making a man aroused?*

A. Yes. In the past, it was thought that testosterone's sexual actions were entirely on the brain. We now know that testosterone also acts directly on the penis and is involved in production of chemical messengers within the erectile chambers that control blood flow, and hence the erection process.

Q. *Does the amount of body hair on a man reflect his testosterone values?*

A. The most important factor influencing body hair is genetics. Men from Asia tend to have relatively little body hair, whereas men of Mediterranean backgrounds tend to have much more. Nevertheless, men who develop low T will often notice that they have lost some of their body hair as well, which will occasionally return with normalization of testosterone. However, raising testosterone levels will not cause body hair to grow in areas it would not have developed normally, like the palms.

Chapter 3

Could You Have Low Testosterone?

Testosterone affects the body in so many ways that it can sometimes be difficult to tell whether someone has low T. Moreover, because many of the symptoms of low T overlap with symptoms of aging, the problem of diagnosing becomes even greater. After all, isn't it normal for men to lose some of their sex drive as they get older? Or to have erections that are not as firm or reliable? Or to feel that they don't have as much get-up-and-go? And when we get to mood issues, such as feeling "blah" or "gray" or even "down," couldn't these all be symptoms of depression rather than low T?

To a certain extent, this is all true. There is no single symptom that absolutely, positively means that someone has low T. And each of the symptoms that are caused by low T can also be caused by other conditions. For that reason, whenever I see a patient who has symptoms that *could* be caused by low T and who has low blood levels of T, I cannot tell him with complete confidence that he has low T syndrome or that treatment will surely relieve his symptoms.

Although I cannot be sure that a patient's symptoms are due to low T or that treatment will help, the questions I ask myself with each such patient are simple: Is it worth seeing whether treatment will help? Is the possibility of benefit greater than the possibility of risk?

I believe the answer is yes. Because low T can be so easily and successfully treated, it is imperative that men who have one or more of the characteristic symptoms undergo evaluation and testing to determine whether they have low T.

In this chapter, I review the symptoms of low T, the signs of low T, and how the diagnosis of low T is made.

What Is Low T?

In this book I've taken the liberty of shortening some technical names and tongue-twisting terminology into the name low T. Because testosterone is measurable in the bloodstream, the term *low T* could simply mean that the levels of testosterone are low (see Chapter 4 for specific information on the blood tests for testosterone and what the results mean). Indeed, low levels of testosterone are an important part of the diagnosis, but the real diagnosis also requires that there be some effect of low T on the person. Such effects may be something that the man notices, such as low sex drive, or it may be something that shows up on tests, such as low bone density or anemia, a low red blood cell count.

The reason for making a distinction between a blood test result showing low levels of testosterone and the condition I call low T is that not all men with low blood levels of testosterone need treatment. At least, with our current state of understanding, there is no solid proof as yet that we should treat them. Let me explain.

One of the primary principles in medicine is that we only intervene, or treat people, when we have reasonable expectations that we will improve their lives, prevent disease, or increase their chances of survival. In general, we refrain from treating people for whom there is no known or proven benefit from the therapy, even if they have a symptom or a test result that is abnormal. Part of the balancing act physicians make every day when making decisions whether to treat someone is that every treatment has potential risks, sometimes known and sometimes unknown. If there's no definite benefit, we tend to withhold treatment, consistent with the medical adage *primum non nocere*, which translates from Latin as "First, do no harm."

When it comes to men who have symptoms from low levels of testosterone, we know there is a very good chance that those symptoms will improve if T levels can be normalized. But one of the curiosities of the field is that there are a large number of men who have blood test results showing low levels of T but have no symptoms whatsoever. Because no one has yet to show convincingly that raising testosterone in these men provides any short- or long-term benefits, there is no reason to treat these men. Thus, having a low level of testosterone is not enough to merit treatment.

This may change as we learn more about testosterone. For instance, several studies over the last few years have shown that men with low testosterone had substantially higher mortality rates than men with normal testosterone levels. This doesn't necessarily mean that those men with low testosterone levels would have lived longer if they had received testosterone therapy, because that possibility wasn't tested in those studies. And it is possible that the low testosterone levels may have simply been an indicator that those men were more likely to have serious illnesses (although the researchers didn't find evidence to support that explanation). These types of results, however, are provocative and raise the possibility that one day we will find reason to treat men with low testosterone levels whether or not they have symptoms.

Nevertheless, at this point I recommend testosterone therapy only for men with low T, defined as the combination of characteristic symptoms or signs and a confirmatory blood test showing reduced levels of testosterone in the blood. These are the men for whom we have evidence there is a reasonable chance of improvement with treatment.

When it comes to diagnosing low T, most texts and experts focus primarily on the blood test results. I take a different view—the emphasis should be on symptoms. The most important part of making the diagnosis is in the listening, in the ability to identify those symptoms suggestive of low T. The greater the number of characteristic symptoms that are present, the more likely the diagnosis will be correct. The blood test is then used to confirm the diagnosis—not the other way around.

As a philosophical point, I believe this is the way medicine works best. There is also the practical issue, which is that the blood test results can be somewhat confusing and even misleading unless one understands what is being measured, as I explain in Chapter 4. Every week in my office, I see happy patients in follow-up who have responded beautifully to testosterone therapy, but who had been told previously by another physician that they couldn't have the condition, because the physician incorrectly believed the lab results were normal. The symptoms are the key, and the blood test results are used to confirm the diagnosis.

Be aware that there are quite a number of other names used for low T in medical literature as well as in publications and websites. The most common is hypogonadism (literally, "underfunctioning testicles"). Androgen deficiency or, more accurately, testosterone deficiency are terms growing in favor. Other terms include late-onset hypogonadism, androgen deficiency in the aging male (ADAM), and partial androgen deficiency of the aging male (PADAM), but I find that these are all too technical and some of them are inaccurate. After all, low T can occur at any age, not just in "aging men," whatever that means. It seems to me that we begin to age from the

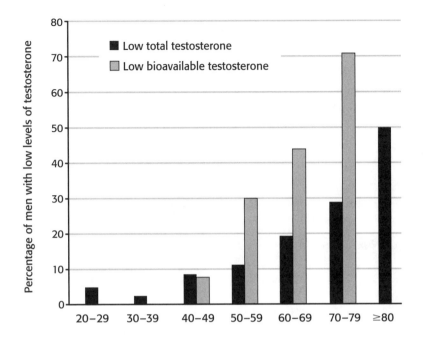

Percentage of Men with Low Testosterone

The percentage of men with low levels of testosterone increases substantially as men age. Shown here is the percentage of men with low testosterone based on measurements of either total testosterone or bioavailable testosterone.

Adapted from E. L. Rhoden and A. Morgentaler, "Risks of Testosterone-Replacement Therapy and Recommendations for Monitoring," *New England Journal of Medicine* 350, (2004): 482–92.

moment we're born—so do I call a thirty-five-year-old man with low testosterone levels an aging man? Thus, the term I use with my patients—and in this book—is low T.

The big picture is that low T is a treatable medical condition caused by a reduction in circulating levels of the hormone testosterone. The diagnosis requires the presence of characteristic symptoms and/or signs, combined with a confirmatory blood test. Let's review the characteristic symptoms to determine if you or a loved one has low T.

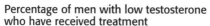

Percentage of men with low testosterone
who have received treatment

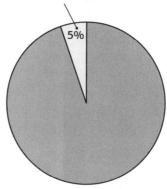

5%

Total Number of American Men with Low Testosterone

Low T is greatly underrecognized and undertreated. According to a recent estimate from the FDA, only 5 percent of American men with low T receive treatment.

Symptoms of Low T

In Chapter 1, I touched on some of the most common sexual and nonsexual symptoms of low T, such as low sex drive, low energy, and erectile dysfunction (ED). The following is a detailed description of how these different symptoms may appear.

Sexual Symptoms

Sex is a complicated process that includes desire, erection, and ejaculation. Testosterone is involved in all of these, so it makes sense that low T can result in a variety of sexual symptoms.

Decreased Desire. The hallmark symptom of low T is decreased libido, also known as low sex drive. Some men with low T, like Jerry, whose story I told in Chapter 1, lose their libido completely, while others just experience a diminished sex drive. One comment I hear frequently from my low T patients is that they do still feel the hunger for sex, and enjoy it very much when it happens, but that the desire for sex just doesn't happen that frequently any more. "Doc, I used to want to have sex every single day and twice on Sunday, but now I'm happy enough to do it once or twice a month," is how I often hear it summarized.

Other men experience the drop in libido differently—desire is still a frequent thought or feeling, but when it occurs it lacks the urgency it once had. As one patient put it, "I still enjoy sex, Doctor, don't get me wrong. And my wife and I still have sex a few times a week, just like we did when we first got married eight years ago. But I don't feel the hunger in the same way. Some nights, if my wife were to tell me she didn't feel up to it for some reason, it would be fine with me. I might even feel relieved. That wasn't true a year ago." This man had noted an overall reduction in the intensity of his sex drive.

It can be difficult sometimes to tell whether a drop in sex drive represents something abnormal or whether it is just a normal part of getting older. And because testosterone levels tend to decline slowly, often over many years, it can be hard to even remember what it was like to have a stronger sex drive. When I ask men whether their sex drive is still strong, it is common for me to hear, "Well, Doctor, it's not like I'm eighteen anymore."

Still, sometimes it can be difficult to sort out what has happened to a man's sex drive, for both the physician and the patient. Gary, a man I treated for low T, had indicated to me at his first visit that his desire for his wife was as strong as the day they had first met twenty-five years ago. When he returned for his first visit after treatment, I asked what he had noticed. He shook his head, smiled sheepishly, and replied, "Doctor, everything is great. But I can't believe how much I think about sex! I'm chasing my wife around the room, just like I used to." When I reminded Gary that he had told me his sex drive was normal at his earlier visit, he nodded and said, "It's true. My desire to have sex with my wife was very strong. But it was a conscious interest, not this . . . ." He searched for the right term, clenched his fist, and smiled, "not this primitive, basic urge."

What Gary was telling me was that when we first spoke about his libido, he was expressing his interest in being sexual again with his wife. But it had been an intellectual idea, not the inner hunger for sex that really gets a guy going. Gary wanted to be able to reclaim his intimacy with his wife, whom he loved very much, and when I asked about his desire level, he answered honestly that he wanted to have sex with his wife. However, once we figured out that we'd been talking about two separate things, intellectual desire to be sexually intimate versus the inner hunger for sex, we discovered in hindsight that Gary's libido had been almost completely absent for two years. Ever since Gary told me his story years ago, I've always been careful to ask about the "hunger for sex" instead of the "desire for sex."

It can be very difficult for a woman to know what to do when a man loses his libido. Many women fear that it is their fault. Some women have told me they feared that their partner's reduced sexual interest was because they were less attractive or perhaps because they had put on weight or aged. Other women have assumed that it was a sign their partner had another lover.

This response is natural, but it can quickly raise the stakes in the bedroom. Not only does the man already feel badly that he may not be "providing" for his partner sexually, but he may also now need to reassure her that he indeed loves her, finds her attractive, and is not cheating on her. He then feels a greater need to perform, to prove he still finds her sexually appealing. But if the feeling isn't there, this can create tremendous stress for a man. His partner may sense he is faking it, or he may find it impossible to achieve or maintain an erection, making the situation even worse.

The best solution is to solve the libido problem, of course. Let's face it—we all feel better when we feel desirable and desired. The good news is that if the problem is related to low T, there is a good chance the problem can be alleviated.

Erectile Dysfunction. A second important symptom of low T is erectile dysfunction (ED). Some men who have ED due to low T, such as Samuel in Chapter 1, have a total inability to achieve any useful erection. Others describe something they find more confusing: "Sometimes I can get a firm erection, and everything goes just the way it should. But too many times, my penis doesn't respond at all. I can't figure out why this is happening. I've paid attention to time of day and what I've eaten. I just don't seem to have any control over it." This intermittent form of ED can be a symptom of low T.

One form of ED that makes me suspect low T is involved is when men describe the need to concentrate or to stay focused to maintain their erection. This contrasts with their previous experiences, in which once they had started sexual play or activity, their erection would stay firm until they had climaxed. One of the primary effects of testosterone in men, as in male mammals and even reptiles, is to work on the centers in the brain that coordinate sexual activity and desire. Usually this drive is so strong that once a male begins sexual activity, it is hard to get distracted by other things, whether it is a human in the bedroom or an animal in the wild. But if testosterone levels are low, these sexual centers in the brain center are less activated, and one may need to deliberately concentrate on the activity to maintain the sexual feeling.

Difficulty Achieving Orgasm. Another symptom of low T can be difficulty achieving an orgasm. Most men would never say that it took "work" to have an orgasm; in fact, a great many men ejaculate more quickly than they would like. But when testosterone is low, the amount of stimulation needed to achieve an orgasm may be greater than usual and can sometimes create difficulties.

Sarah, the wife of one of my patients, Alexi, piped up during our initial meeting—before Alexi had a chance to finish describing his symptoms. "I never knew that a man could have sex and not be able to finish," she said. "When we first married, there was no problem. Now, for the last year, it takes him forever to finish, and sometimes I even think he fakes it!" Although Alexi did not admit to faking it, men with low T have certainly shared with me that they have done so.

Some of these men with low T get close to the feeling that they are about to have an ejaculation but need to draw on particularly exciting fantasies or thoughts to "get over the hump." Some men only rarely achieve orgasm with sex but have no problem with masturbation. This sounds psychological, and it may certainly be so in cases where the man has intimacy issues. In other cases, however, it is because the threshold to achieve orgasm is higher when testosterone is low and requires a special kind of stimulation that is impossible during intercourse.

This difficulty achieving an orgasm has a medical name that struck me as enormously funny (although politically incorrect) when I was in medical school—retarded ejaculation. Other causes of retarded ejaculation include diabetes, neurological disorders such as multiple sclerosis, poor nerve function or sensation in the genital region from any condition, psychological issues, and medications. Medications are by far the most common culprits for this, particularly the selective serotonin reuptake inhibitors, such as Prozac, Paxil, and Zoloft, that are used to treat depression or anxiety disorders. Psychological causes tend to be long-standing, usually lifelong, and related to fear of loss of control or fear of becoming a father. However, when a man describes this symptom as a relatively new event occurring within a stable relationship, and in the absence of troublesome medications, low T should be considered a likely culprit.

Reduced Amount of Ejaculatory Fluid. When a man ejaculates, the fluid expelled is a combination of secretions that come primarily from three organs—the prostate, the seminal vesicles (which lie just behind the prostate), and the testicular fluid that includes the sperm. All three of these structures—prostate, seminal vesicles, and testicles—are under the control of testosterone. When levels of testosterone are low, the production of fluid by these organs can be diminished. It usually requires quite low levels of testosterone to cause this reduction in fluid.

There can be other causes of reduced ejaculatory volume. Nearly all men lose the pulsatile spurting of ejaculatory fluid that accompanies orgasm as they enter their thirties or forties, with fluid coming out more slowly and sometimes just oozing out. This may seem to be a reduced amount of total fluid, but the total amount may not be any different. Some men, particularly diabetics, may have some of the fluid enter into the nearby bladder, a condition called retrograde ejaculation, where it is expelled with the next urination. Not surprisingly, retrograde ejaculation also can cause problems with fertility. Some men may have restricted fluid expulsion due to partial blockages of the urine passageway from strictures or even an enlarged prostate. Medications used to treat an enlarged prostate, called alpha blockers, can also reduce the volume of semen.

Reduced Intensity of the Orgasm. There is an old joke that goes like this:

Q: "Why do men want sex so much?"
A: "Because it feels good."

The joke is based on the obvious. Sex feels good, so we want to do it. And although there may be many aspects of sex that are experienced as pleasurable, for the most part, the payoff is the orgasm—the feeling of "bells and whistles" or of the "earth moving" as Hemingway described it in *For Whom the Bell Tolls*.

Yet for some men with low T, the orgasm stops being the amazing experience it once was: "Doctor, it used to be that when I had an orgasm, it was a huge 'WOW!' every time. But recently, the feeling is so dulled that sometimes I can't even tell if I've finished." This is definitely *not* a normal description of an orgasm. And often it is an indication of low T.

Nonsexual Symptoms of Low T

Although the sexual effects of low T are common and affect men profoundly, for many men it is the nonsexual symptoms of low T that really disturb them. Even if T therapy hasn't caused as much improvement in sexual symptoms as we would like, often patients wish to continue with treatment because of the other benefits they've gained, such as improved mood or sense of well-being. Let's review these other symptoms of low T.

Low Energy or Increased Fatigue. These two symptoms often occur together. Low energy may seem to be the same as fatigue, but they differ in a subtle way. When we speak of being energetic or having energy, it refers to the way that we bring a sense of enthusiasm to a project or to having enough "oomph" to get things done. When men complain that their energy is low, they may describe examples such as "My couch speaks to me," or "I've always had issues with my posture, so I usually try to stand up straight, even though it's a conscious effort for me. But recently I haven't been doing that. I don't seem to have the energy."

Perhaps more commonly, men describe this lack of energy as affecting their work or their activities at home. "I don't participate in meetings at work the way I once did," or "I've always liked going out after work with my coworkers, but now I just don't have the energy for it." Or "I've gone from being an active guy on the weekends to someone who just sits on the couch watching TV."

The sense of increased fatigue that can accompany low T is a little more specific. "I feel tired all the time," is one frequent description. Another is "I've started taking naps after meals." Now, I'm as big a fan of naps as the next guy, and by itself the enjoyment of a nap doesn't indicate much of anything. The point is that when this is something new in someone's life, or if the feeling is more common than he'd experienced before, then it may be a significant indicator of low T.

Loss of Motivation. Motivation is the way we approach the things we do. In some cases, it describes whether we have some degree of passion for our work, our relationships, or our lives in general. Although motivation can be affected by fatigue or a sense of low energy, motivation itself has a somewhat different meaning and can be a symptom of low T.

Effects of Low T on Mood. There are two different ways that low T can affect mood negatively. One is that a man feels less upbeat, with less enjoyment of life. Some men will experience this as "the blahs." They just don't get excited about stuff—no laughing or fun. Activities that once gave them pleasure are now just so-so. The other problem with mood may be more obvious. Men in this situation may describe feeling down or blue or having a short fuse, something the experts call irritability.

Mood can be a difficult thing to get a handle on, because it varies so much depending on circumstances. Everyone has experienced having a great day, followed by a day when everything seems lousy, even though no special events have occurred. These are just the vicissitudes of life. And when there are troubling events in our lives, such as an illness, a work-related problem, or a family problem, it is only natural to experience negative feelings, regardless of one's hormone levels. When I am determining whether someone has mood changes that may be related to low T, I ask questions that deal with an overall assessment of a significant period of time, such as, "Over the last few months, have you been as upbeat as you once were?"

Obviously, if there are important issues happening at that moment in a man's life, it may be impossible to get a handle on whether his mood is being affected. In this case, the best thing to do is to wait until the situation has resolved. Examples include health issues for the man or his family, stressful business or work-related events, or the death of someone close. It is important to recognize that life has its ups and downs that can strongly influence our moods, even when hormone levels are perfectly normal.

Overall Sense of Well-Being or Vigor. One of the things some men with low T have difficulty putting their fingers on is their overall sense of how they feel. What do we call it when life is fine and there are no issues, but we just don't have the sense of being on top of the world? Sometimes, the only way to know that things aren't right is when we feel the difference.

And so it was when I first started treating men with low T and saw them back in follow-up in the office. As much as testosterone therapy can be useful for men with sexual symptoms, it doesn't always work, but it can help with other symptoms. This was the case for Kyle, a fifty-two-year-old electrician. Three months of T therapy hadn't worked to help with Kyle's erections, so I suggested we discontinue the testosterone and try something else. Kyle listened to me patiently. When I was finished speaking, he said, "Doctor, if it's all right with you, I'd like to continue with the testosterone, and I'd be happy to try the new treatment, too." When I asked why he wanted to continue even though the testosterone treatment hadn't helped with his erections, he told me, "I just feel better ever since I started the testosterone. More vigorous. My wife tells me I have a different look about me, and although I can't describe it to you exactly, I know just what she's saying. There's more bounce to my step. I guess the best way to put it is that I just feel good."

Loss of One's "Mojo." Several of the items I've listed in this section are what we call soft symptoms, meaning that they are hard to define and hard to measure, and thus it is hard to know whether they have improved with treatment. For this reason, through most of my career, I've been reluctant to prescribe treatment or even suggest there may be a problem with testosterone unless a man has had more specific symptoms.

However, after having so very many men come back to my office with their stories after T treatment, I'm convinced that these subtle soft symptoms have a great deal to do with a man's quality of life and with his sense of himself as a vigorous person. Perhaps another way to put it is that some of these men wind up feeling more like a man.

Men know when they feel on top of their game. When they feel like they have their "mojo" working. When they feel like they are the male lion roaring as king of the jungle. Now, socially, human males don't really roar, and they're not supposed to strut like roosters either. But they do know when they feel like the king of the castle, even when that castle is just their own small corner of the universe. Whether this is mood, or vigor, or sense of well-being, or energy—who's to say? But there's something about all of this that just feels right to a man. Men know it when they feel it. The loss of that feeling is common with low T, and treatment can bring it back.

Signs of Low T

In the previous sections, I've described the various symptoms of low T, and in the following section I describe the signs of low T. The difference, as mentioned before, is that symptoms are something a person experiences, and signs are something that can be measured, like weight or height or blood pressure.

Loss of Muscle Strength and Mass

In the past, it was unusual for a man to know whether the amount of muscle on his body had changed or whether he had lost an appreciable amount of strength. But with so many men working out regularly, it is not unusual now for men to tell me, "I used to be able to bench-press 220 pounds, and now I can't even do 180 pounds." Or "I know how my body responds to exercise and how quickly I can move up on the weights when I'm in training, but over the last year, I've just been stuck at the same weights. My body isn't responding to exercise the way it used to." Like Jack from Chapter 1, these men notice a marked difference in their overall physical performance.

Golfers have their own way of measuring these things. It's not uncommon for me to hear from healthy, fit men, "I'm not getting the same distance from my driver," or "I now need an extra club or two to reach the par 3s." It's not as if men with low T become instant weaklings. But in situations where they are able to measure their strength against their own standards, they find they have lost something.

Not surprisingly, men who do work out or exercise regularly tend to be quite pleased with their muscular response to exercise when their testosterone is normalized again.

Accumulation of Fat

Raising testosterone in men with low T has consistently been shown to lower the percentage and amount of body fat. Sometimes a particularly fit individual with low T will complain that no matter how much he exercises, he just can't get rid of the fat around his waist. Although this can be due simply to aging, it may also be a sign of low T. Usually, this fat accumulation has been a slow, gradual process if it is related to low T. Sudden weight gain or rapid fluctuations in weight are *not* indicative of low T.

An interesting relationship that has not been completely characterized is the interplay between testosterone, diabetes, and obesity. A very high percentage of men who develop diabetes as an adult are overweight or obese; in turn, as many as one-third of diabetic men have low T concentrations. Even more interesting is the observation that a low T concentration increases the risk of being diagnosed with diabetes sometime in the future. Normalizing testosterone causes a reduction in the amount of fat in the body and can also help with blood sugar control.

Low Bone Density

People would never know they had low bone density unless they had it measured, suffered a fracture due to an unusually mild amount of force or injury, or had x-rays obtained for some other reason that suggested the bone was not particularly dense. Low bone density is called osteopenia when the loss of bone is mild and osteoporosis when it is more severe.

Several studies have shown that low T is associated with reduced bone density in men and that testosterone treatment can reverse this. This effect is quite slow, however, as is all treatment for low bone density. The effects may differ for different bone areas, such as the spine and the hip. Men with low T should be tested regularly for bone density: at the time of diagnosis and every two years thereafter if the first test is normal. If bone density is low, yearly examinations should be obtained to monitor progress. Men with osteoporosis should consult their physician or be referred to a specialist for optimal management, which will usually involve treatments instead of, or in addition to, testosterone supplementation.

Anemia

Our red blood cells are critical for life because of their function of carrying oxygen to our tissues. The average red blood cell lives approximately one hundred days, so the supply must be continually replenished by our bone marrow. When the red blood cell count is low, it is common to feel tired or, in severe cases, to experience shortness of breath with minor exertion. The condition of having low levels of red blood cells is called anemia. It has multiple causes, including deficiencies of iron, folate, or vitamin B_{12}, as well as bleeding from the intestinal tract.

If a physician finds that a man is anemic, there are certain things he automatically tests for, such as iron or folate deficiencies. Yet a certain number of individuals will have anemia without any known cause. And some of these men will have low T as the cause of their anemia. But because this relationship is not widely known, it has not yet become a standard to check for low T in cases of anemia. In my practice, there are several dozen men whose anemia had been considered a mystery by their physicians and whose blood counts normalized with testosterone treatment. This information about testosterone and anemia is slowly reaching the wider medical community.

Confirming the Diagnosis

The number of symptoms and signs of low T are many, and it may therefore not be obvious to a man or his physician that his symptoms are pointing to low T as the diagnosis. An added source of confusion is that many of the symptoms overlap with symptoms of depression or with what we consider normal aging. The main point to make about this is that if the symptoms are due to low T, they will respond to treatment. In contrast, the diagnosis of aging does not improve with T therapy. If you or a loved one has one or more of the symptoms or signs described in this section, the next step is to have blood tests obtained to determine whether testosterone levels are indeed low.

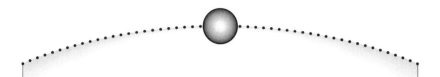

Questions and Answers

Q. *Isn't it possible that my loss of interest in sex is due to depression?*

A. Depression is certainly associated with loss of libido, as well as other symptoms of low T, such as lack of motivation and feeling less upbeat. Despite this overlap between depression and low T, I typically do not find these conditions difficult to distinguish from each other. The loss of libido due to low T usually occurs without any other important symptoms of depression. On the other hand, if a man is feeling persistently sad, rather than just blah; feels hopeless, worthless, and helpless; or has thoughts about suicide or hurting others, then this sounds like true depression and requires urgent attention from a mental health professional.

Q. *At the gym, I have never been able to achieve the same kind of muscle definition as other men. Could this be due to low T?*

A. If this has been a lifelong condition, this is more likely due to how your body is built rather than to low T. However, if a man finds that he no longer has the muscular response to exercise that he once had, then it may be worthwhile to see if his testosterone is low.

Q. *I've put on forty pounds over the last year. Is this a sign of low T?*

A. Not when there is so much weight involved. Low T can affect fat accumulation and distribution, but usually to a mild degree.

Q. *My wife and I are now in our early fifties and have been married for over twenty-five years. Now that the children are grown and out of the house, she's become much more interested in sex and complains that my sex drive has diminished because we have sex only once or twice each week. This is no different than it's been for many, many years. I very much enjoy sex when we have it, but her appetite for sex has increased. Do I really have a low sex drive?*

A. It doesn't sound like it. There is no such thing as a normal amount of sex drive, because there is so much variation from one individual to another. Some individuals are unhappy when they have sex less than once each day, whereas others are perfectly content with sex every two weeks or so. A common challenge within relationships is when one partner desires sex more frequently than the other. One solution is to find creative ways to sexually satisfy the partner with the greater drive in between episodes of actual sexual intercourse. And enjoy the fact that your wife is almost certainly sexually available when you do have the urge to play.

Q. *I've been feeling less motivated, with less get-up-and-go, ever since my diabetes was diagnosed three years ago. My doctor thought I might be depressed, but antidepressants didn't help and I stopped them. My wife says it's just a normal part of having a chronic medical condition like diabetes. Could my symptoms be due to low T?*

A. Yes, it's certainly possible, and it's definitely worth investigating. There can be many reasons why a man may feel less vigorous or motivated, but the value in determining whether low T is present is that it can be successfully treated. Low T is also frequently found in men with diabetes or many other chronic conditions. Ask your doctor to obtain a blood test for testosterone.

Chapter 4

What You Should Know About Being Evaluated for Low Testosterone

Now that you or your physician has determined that you have the symptoms or signs of low T, it is time to figure out whether you really have this condition. For this, it is necessary to do a blood test.

The diagnosis of low T can be straightforward if the blood test shows very low levels of T. But for many men with low T, the process of getting the proper diagnosis based on blood test results can be confusing and frustrating. If this has happened to you, it is not your doctor's fault. Somehow, medical "wisdom" has generated so many mixed messages about the diagnosis that the average physician finds it very difficult to determine if a patient truly has low T. Nevertheless, the diagnosis can be made easily enough if one understands some basic information about testosterone and the various available tests.

Once or twice a week, I see men with low T who have been told by other physicians that their testosterone levels were normal. Felipe was a good example. A forty-seven-year-old man with his own landscaping business, Felipe had worked hard and now had a good-sized crew of men working for him. Business was good. But for the last six months he had just felt tired all the time and lacked motivation. "I'm happy when it rains these days, because then I don't have to go to work—I just roll over and go back to sleep," Felipe admitted. He said that his sex drive was reduced, but he attributed this to his fatigue: "I just don't have the energy for sex like I used to, if you can believe it."

Felipe's primary care physician wondered if he might have low T and had obtained the standard test, called total testosterone, or total T, which showed a level of 410 ng/dL. His doctor told Felipe that this level was very normal, and therefore his problem could not be due to low T. Felipe's physician discussed with him the possibility that perhaps he was depressed or not getting enough sleep. Felipe was certain these weren't the cause of his problem.

When I repeated Felipe's blood tests, his total T was 420 ng/dL, a value very similar to the last one and well within what is considered the normal range, which is usually listed as between 300 and 1,000 ng/dL. However, the level of his free testosterone, or free T, was markedly reduced, at 8.4 pg/mL. Free T reflects the biologically active form of testosterone, and it can be reduced in men with low T even when the more common test, total T, is entirely normal (this is described later in this chapter). But the important point for Felipe was that his blood tests confirmed a diagnosis of low T, despite a normal total T. Felipe responded nicely to testosterone treatment. Within a month, he was back to building up his business. "Now on rainy days," Felipe told me, "I make the rounds of various businesses in the area, trying to drum up new accounts."

Felipe's story underscores the importance of understanding the various testosterone blood tests and of knowing how to interpret them. It is not at all unusual for a man with treatable symptoms of low T to have a testosterone result that appears normal, especially if that test is for total testosterone.

To avoid the hurdles of laboratory misdiagnosis, there are several issues that need to be addressed:

- Which tests should be ordered and why?
- How should you and your doctor interpret results of those tests?
- What results are consistent with low T?
- What are normal and abnormal values?
- Under what circumstances are additional tests required?
- Can I trust the values for "normal" provided by the local laboratory?

Understanding the Various Blood Tests

There are so many blood tests to measure testosterone that it is no wonder most physicians are confused about which ones to order and how to interpret them. These tests include total testosterone and free testosterone, which I've already mentioned, as well as bioavailable testosterone, free androgen index, calculated free testosterone, free and weakly bound testosterone, and percent free testosterone. To understand the value of these tests and why some tests are more useful than others, it is helpful to review how testosterone travels in the circulation.

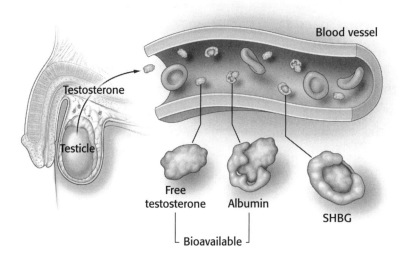

How Testosterone Circulates in the Bloodstream

Testosterone is produced within the testicles and is then released into the bloodstream to reach distant parts of the body. Testosterone circulates in three primary forms: (1) attached to sex hormone–binding globulin (SHBG), (2) attached to albumin, or (3) unattached (free). The binding of testosterone to SHBG is so tight that this portion is not considered bioavailable. In contrast, the testosterone molecule is only weakly bound to albumin, making it readily available to cells that need it. The unbound, or free, testosterone is similarly available to cells. Blood tests for total testosterone will measure all three of these fractions, but bioavailable testosterone consists only of the portion that is free and the portion bound to albumin.

Approximately 95 percent of testosterone is made by the testicles, with the remainder produced by the adrenal glands, situated above the kidneys. Once produced by the testicles, testosterone is secreted into the bloodstream, where it can then reach any other location within the body where it is needed. Like a number of other hormones, the majority of testosterone travels in the bloodstream bound to carrier molecules, which act as a reservoir for testosterone and protect it from being degraded by other enzymes in the bloodstream.

Almost all testosterone in the circulation is bound to these carrier proteins, leaving only about 1–2 percent of testosterone to float freely in the circulation, unbound to any other molecule. This unbound portion is called free testosterone. Two proteins in particular are responsible for binding the bulk of testosterone in the circulation. The first is a special carrier molecule called sex hormone–binding globulin, usually referred to by its abbreviation, SHBG. The other major carrier molecule for testosterone is albumin, which is the most plentiful protein in the bloodstream.

A key characteristic of the binding of SHBG to testosterone is that it is so tight that essentially none of the bound T is available to enter the cells where it does its work. This portion of testosterone that is bound to SHBG is thus not bioavailable. In contrast, the binding of testosterone to albumin is weak, allowing testosterone to free itself from this carrier protein and make itself available to cells as needed.

These characteristics help to explain what is being measured by the various testosterone blood tests. Total testosterone refers to the entire amount of testosterone detected in the blood, whether free or attached to carrier molecules such as SHBG and albumin. Bioavailable testosterone refers to the free portion and the testosterone that is bound to albumin. And free testosterone refers only to the unbound portion.

Which Test Is Best?

Now that you understand how testosterone is circulated throughout the body, let's take a closer look at the different tests.

Total Testosterone

Total testosterone was the first test for testosterone. It is simple to measure and has been the standard test used for several decades. For this reason, all physicians are familiar with it, having learned about it during medical training. In fact, whenever physicians say, "The testosterone level was X," they are referring in a kind of shorthand to total testosterone. Just about every study on testosterone ever published has included total T measurements, even when the focus has been on measurements of bioavailable or free T. In addition, nearly all textbooks and published guidelines or recommendations focus on total T values. So it is easy to understand why most physicians only order a total T blood test when a man is suspected to have low T.

Total T can be a very useful test, but in many cases it is terribly misleading. As I already mentioned, a large proportion of what is measured by total T is inactive, due to testosterone's tight binding to SHBG. If a man has high SHBG levels, this will tend to make his total T appear normal, even though he may truly have low levels of bioavailable testosterone. And because SHBG increases with age, total testosterone becomes less reliable in older men, which is the very age group at greatest risk for having low T. The concept that a man can have normal-appearing total T yet be symptomatic because there are low levels of testosterone available to his body's cells is a critical point that has not yet filtered down to the wider medical community. This "blind spot" has resulted in a great many men with low T being told they have normal testosterone levels and thus being denied a potentially beneficial treatment. This is exactly what happened to Felipe.

Despite this, the total T test should not be entirely dismissed. In most cases, total T does properly reflect the testosterone status of a man. And in particular, when total T is low, there should be no doubt that a man truly has low T.

Bioactive or Bioavailable Testosterone

Theoretically, bioavailable testosterone would seem to be the best test, but there are technical issues with how the test is performed that makes it less useful and practical. This is usually an indirect blood test, derived from other test results, and it currently has few advocates as the best indicator of low T. Some labs will report a test as "free and weakly bound testosterone," which is another way of describing bioavailable testosterone. For the most part, the use of the bioavailable T test has been replaced by the free T blood test, which is simpler and more directly measured and accurately reflects whether there are low or normal amounts of useful testosterone within the body.

Free Testosterone

There is general agreement among experts—at least in theory—that free testosterone is the best indicator of a man's testosterone status. But there is much less agreement regarding the value of the various types of tests used to measure free T. Although free T makes up only 1–2 percent of the total circulating testosterone in the body, it serves as an excellent marker for what is available to the cells.

A number of tests have been used to measure free T, but there has been so much controversy over the quality and interpretation of these various tests that many community physicians have given up on free T and depend primarily or exclusively on total T. This is a shame, because free T is the best test to determine if a man truly has low T. In the following sections, I give some details on these free T tests because I feel so strongly that free T is the best test to identify low T in a man. It is therefore worthwhile to know something about the controversy and the relative merits of these tests.

Analog Free T. The free T test I use and recommend is called the analog free T test. (It is also commonly called a RIA test.) This test can be ordered from nearly every doctor's office, laboratory, clinic, or hospital in the country, and it is easy to use and interpret. The results correspond nicely with whether someone has low T at the time of diagnosis, as well as whether testosterone levels respond adequately during treatment. In fact, it was the analog free T result that helped me diagnose Felipe's low T.

Unfortunately, the analog free T test has gained an undeservedly bad reputation for being unreliable, and its use has been discouraged by some experts. The criticism of the analog free T test stems from studies showing that this test provides much lower results than another test for free T called equilibrium dialysis, which is a labor-intensive technique that has been considered the gold standard by laboratory researchers.

In a key study by Dr. Alex Vermeulen and coworkers, various tests for free T were compared using the same blood samples from human subjects. The study used equilibrium dialysis as the standard, and results from the other tests were compared to equilibrium dialysis results to see how well they performed. A test called calculated free T gave an excellent correlation to equilibrium dialysis and was declared the winner. The analog free T test also correlated extremely well, but it gave much lower values and, for this reason, was dismissed by the authors as inaccurate.

For every increase in equilibrium dialysis, however, there was a proportional increase in results for the analog free T test. This is like comparing temperatures in Fahrenheit and centigrade. The values in centigrade are always lower than Fahrenheit (e.g., the freezing point for water is 32° Fahrenheit and 0° centigrade), but the information is equivalent. The only important difference is that a different scale is used. This is why we already use a lower

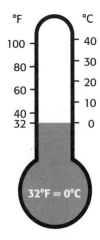

Tests for Free Testosterone

The most commonly available laboratory test for free testosterone (the analog free T assay) has been criticized because it provides numbers that are lower than those provided by tests favored by some experts (equilibrium dialysis and calculated free T). However, because high correlation between these tests is so strong, all the tests give the same information, just like reading a temperature in centigrade instead of Fahrenheit.

scale for the analog free T test to determine which results are normal and which are low.

Equilibrium Dialysis. Equilibrium dialysis is an excellent laboratory technique, but it requires a lot of time and human labor, unlike almost all other lab tests (including the analog free T test) that are performed rapidly and automatically by machines. Although this test is often described as the best by various experts and texts, the unfortunate fact is that it is not available to the average patient or his doctor. In a survey of twenty-four academic and community hospital laboratories, not one offered equilibrium dialysis. A national laboratory did make the test available, but only by special request.

In the end, it doesn't much matter if equilibrium dialysis is best, because the only ones who use it are researchers.

Calculated Free T. Calculated free T is a measurement that comes from knowing the values for total T, SHBG, and albumin. These values are plugged into a computer program, which then calculates the result based on an established equation. Results of the calculated free T correspond well with equilibrium dialysis. To get the results, however, it is necessary to find a free T "calculator" online. One that is easy to use can be found at the website for the International Society for the Study of the Aging Male at issam.ch/freetesto.htm. Values for total T, SHBG, and albumin (optional) are inputted, and the website then yields the result.

The calculated free T test is a good test, but it is somewhat impractical. To get the result, I need to take the lab report for my patient, go to my computer, find the website, put in the test results, and then copy down the calculated free T value. There's nothing wrong with this, but I find no need for it in my practice, because the analog free T test provides me with essentially the same information and doesn't require any extra steps. A study of our data conducted by one of my colleagues, Dr. Anita Shyam, won a prize at the 2007 meeting of the Sexual Medicine Society of North America for showing that the results of the analog free T test correlated strongly with those of the calculated free T test.

Free Androgen Index. The free androgen index (FAI) was developed as another attempt to get a handle on free testosterone values. The FAI is a ratio, obtained by dividing the concentration of total T by the concentration of SHBG. It became popular several years ago as a test that would reflect bioavailable T, but its use has been largely abandoned because no one really knows what is being measured by this ratio of total T to SHBG. It has not shown any great clinical usefulness.

How Can I Tell If My Testosterone Levels Are Low?

The average concentration of total T in men over forty years old is approximately 450 ng/dL, and is somewhat higher in younger men. Among healthy young men in their twenties or thirties, it is uncommon to see results that are lower than 350 ng/dL or higher than 800 ng/dL. However, testosterone concentrations decline with age beginning in the mid- to late thirties, by approximately 1 percent per year, or 10 percent per decade. Thus we see more and more men in their fifties and sixties with total testosterone levels below anything seen in younger healthy men.

One study looked at the percentage of men in each decade of life (e.g., forties and fifties) who had bioavailable T levels below the concentrations seen in a group of healthy men in their twenties. If we use the lowest level seen among the twenty-year-olds as the bottom value for what we would consider normal, then approximately 10 percent of forty-year-olds, 20 percent of fifty-year-olds, and 30 percent of sixty-year-olds had reduced levels of T.

However, many men with low concentrations of testosterone have no symptoms or signs of low T. They feel just fine, thank you. And although one day we might learn that it is beneficial for these men to receive testosterone treatment as a preventive measure, for the moment there is little reason to diagnose these men with low T or to suggest that they deserve treatment. On the other hand, my practice is full of men whose total T values seemed normal but whose symptoms were entirely consistent with low T. This overlap of T values in men with and without symptoms has made it impossible to come up with a specific value that accurately and reliably distinguishes men who meet the criteria for low T (and may benefit from treatment) from those who do not (and for whom treatment will not provide any benefits).

Nonetheless, the practical situation is fairly simple and straightforward, because we really only need to concern ourselves with men who have symptoms of low T. If a man has characteristic symptoms or signs of low T and has low or borderline levels of total T or free T, then he deserves a trial of testosterone therapy.

What Is a Low Level of Testosterone?

There is no consensus as to what level of testosterone should be considered low and therefore merit a trial of treatment. In a set of guidelines published in 2006 by the well-respected Endocrine Society, the authors of the guidelines wrote that it is impossible to find a single testosterone value that reliably separates men without symptoms of low T from men with symptoms of low T. Yet, to provide some guidance on this issue, the authors chose the value of 300 ng/dL as their threshold, coinciding with the value used by the U.S. Food and Drug Administration (FDA) to define testosterone deficiency.

This means that, for the authors of the guidelines and for the FDA, a man with a total T of 301 ng/dL does not have low T, whereas a man with a total T of 299 ng/dL does have low T. Obviously, in the real world, this narrow distinction doesn't work very well, particularly because there can be variation in the total T result by as much as 50–75 ng/dL, even from the same blood sample. For this reason, I believe it is far preferable to recommend ranges of results, as recommended by the Second Andropause Consensus Panel (of which I was a member) and based on the observation that the likelihood of true low T increases with decreasing levels of testosterone. The recommendations of the panel were as follows:

Low T is unlikely for total T values above 400 ng/dL.

Low T is definitely present if testosterone is below 200 ng/dL.

A diagnosis of low T is possible and requires clinical judgment if testosterone is between 200 ng/dL and 400 ng/dL.

My own view is that total T concentrations of less than 400 ng/dL are suspicious, concentrations of less than 350 ng/dL are highly suggestive, and values of less than 300 ng/dL should be considered definitely low.

Despite all this emphasis on total T, there is general agreement that free T is more important, due to the possibility that high SHBG tends to make total T appear normal. In my practice, I primarily use the free T test result to decide whether a man is a candidate for treatment. Although in most cases, the total T and free T results will tell the same story, it is not all that unusual for a man to have an impressively low free T result and a total T greater than 400 ng/dL, due to a generous SHBG concentration. It is exactly because of the wide variation in SHBG (which affects total T but not free T) that I rely primarily on the free T result and offer treatment if free T is low and total T appears to be normal.

In my practice, free T concentrations below 15 pg/mL are considered consistent with low T when determined by the analog free T test (this is almost always the test performed when the physician orders free T). For free T determined by equilibrium dialysis or calculated free T, values below 50 pg/mL are considered to be low.

What Does It Mean If Total and Free T Concentrations Do Not Agree?

I have mentioned already that there is uniform agreement that free T more accurately reflects the body's testosterone status than total T does, due to the fact that a large proportion of the circulating testosterone is not biologically available. Despite this fact, the familiarity that most physicians have with total T—and thus their reliance on this test—appears to frequently trump a logical conclusion when total T and free T do not agree.

Felipe's case is a perfect example of this. His total T was in the normal range, above 400 ng/dL, yet his free T was quite low, at 8.4 pg/mL (normal is > than 15 pg/mL). Many physicians are uncomfortable saying that a situation like this merits T therapy, even though they know in theory that a high SHBG can cause total T to look normal in a man with low levels of free T. In fact, Felipe did have a high SHBG concentration. There is no mystery in this case to explain the difference in results between a normal total T and a low level of free T. It is just that many physicians are not yet comfortable enough to diagnose low T when the total T looks normal.

The bottom line is this: if a man has symptoms and has low levels of either total T or free T, he has low T, and a trial of treatment should be considered.

Laboratory Reports and "Normal" Values for Testosterone

There is an additional common problem in interpreting testosterone results, which is that nearly all laboratories provide a range of normal values for total or free T that have nothing to do with the diagnosis of low T. The reason is that these reference values categorize the lowest 2.5 percent of results as low and the highest 2.5 percent of values as high, without any regard for symptoms and without any input from experts who deal with low T. Categorizing blood test results as high or low in this way is standard operating procedure, and this statistical approach applies to almost all blood tests, with only rare exceptions, such as for blood sugar or cholesterol.

To give an example, my own hospital's laboratory provides a normal range for total T of 270–800 ng/dL. This is because the manufacturer of the blood test used by the hospital laboratory recommended this range based on an internal study in which 2.5 percent of the men they studied had test results below this range and 2.5 percent had values above this range. No one asked any of these men if they had any symptoms of low T. This means that a result of 280 ng/dL would be categorized by the lab as normal, even though most experts would consider this value to be quite low. This can obviously be quite confusing for physicians, who tend to rely on their local laboratory's determination of whether a result is normal or abnormal.

An additional problem is that it seems nearly every laboratory has its own set of values for what is normal. In the study of academic and community hospital laboratories I mentioned previously, my colleagues and I discovered seventeen different sets of "normal" values among twenty-five laboratories!

As a rule, laboratory reports tend to categorize too many low or borderline total T and free T results as normal. On the other hand, if a total T or free T value is categorized as low by a laboratory report, it is almost certain that this is correct.

For these reasons, it is important for you to be familiar with the ranges of testosterone that are considered normal and low. Ask to see your lab results, and be sure to discuss them with your doctor.

What Tests Should Be Obtained in the Evaluation of Low T?

If you think you might have low T, you should have two blood tests obtained:

- Total T
- Free T

If either one is low (total T $<$ 350 ng/dL and, especially, free T $<$ 15 pg/mL), then there is a strong possibility that you have low T and might benefit from treatment. This also means that your doctor should obtain a few additional tests to look for a possible explanation of the low T, because there are safety issues that need to be monitored if you begin T therapy.

These additional tests are the following:

- Luteinizing hormone (LH)
- Prolactin
- Hematocrit or hemoglobin
- Prostate-specific antigen (PSA)
- Bone density

Luteinizing Hormone

LH levels will show whether your pituitary gland is working properly to regulate and stimulate testosterone production. Low levels raise the possibility of a problem with the pituitary gland or hypothalamus, and additional tests may be necessary to evaluate this. High levels mean that the problem has arisen because the testicles are unable to produce testosterone adequately despite a strong stimulus to do so. Most men who have what we call "the low T of aging" will have an LH level that is within the normal range. One of the key concepts recognized over the last ten years or so is that the decline in testosterone seen with advancing age is associated in most cases with normal LH levels. Just because low T becomes increasingly common with age, with or without abnormal LH concentrations, does not mean it should be dismissed. Regardless of the reason it occurs, men with low T stand a good chance of responding positively to treatment.

Prolactin

Very high levels of prolactin may reveal the presence of a tumor of the pituitary gland, which in turn can cause low T. Fortunately, these tumors are rare and not malignant. Minor elevations in prolactin are common and without medical significance, but men who have prolactin concentrations more than twice the normal level should undergo imaging of their pituitary glands with an MRI.

Hematocrit and Hemoglobin

The hematocrit and hemoglobin tests indicate whether there are normal numbers of red blood cells in the bloodstream. Low T can contribute to low values, called anemia, and T therapy can also stimulate production of excessive numbers of red blood cells, called erythrocytosis. This test should be obtained as a baseline and then again during T therapy to make sure the hematocrit and hemoglobin values don't rise too high.

Prostate-Specific Antigen (PSA)

PSA is a chemical that is made by a normal prostate and can be detected in blood. Many conditions can raise the PSA, but the one we worry about most is prostate cancer. In Chapter 7, I describe the relationship of testosterone to prostate cancer in greater detail. A PSA should be obtained to have a baseline value prior to beginning testosterone treatment and to make sure it is not too high to begin with.

If the PSA is high, it is important to have a prostate biopsy to make sure there is no hidden cancer present. This holds true whether or not a man has low T and whether or not he plans to take T therapy.

Bone Density

Bone density testing is recommended in men with low T because of the association with osteoporosis or osteopenia. The test is simple, is noninvasive, and takes only a few minutes to perform. If bone density is low, the test should be repeated yearly. If normal, it is sufficient to repeat the test every two years. Testosterone therapy has been shown to cause improvement in bone density, but it may take one or more years of treatment to see a significant change in results.

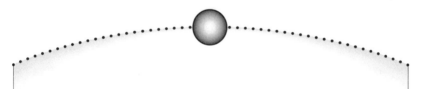

Questions and Answers

Q. *Does the time of day of the blood test matter?*

A. A standard recommendation for many years has been to obtain testosterone blood tests in the early morning, prior to 10:00 A.M., because this is when levels are highest. Some physicians will therefore ask their afternoon patients to return early the next morning to have their blood drawn. However, this is unnecessary.

Large changes in testosterone concentrations during the course of the day have been shown to occur only in young, healthy men under the age of forty years. In a study of 3,006 men, average testosterone concentrations were unchanged from 6:00 A.M. through 2:00 P.M., then declined by a modest 13 percent from 2:00 to 6:00 P.M. This degree of change is unlikely to alter the diagnosis of low T. Moreover, there was evidence to suggest that men with testosterone levels of 300 ng/dL or less—the men who are likely to be diagnosed with low T—had even less variation over the course of the day. In my practice, I obtain blood tests at whatever time of day the man appears in my office for his appointment, whether it is morning or afternoon.

Q. *Do low T levels need to be repeated to confirm the diagnosis?*

A. I repeat blood tests only when the results do not seem to fit the medical picture or when they are surprising. If a man has very low libido and his T levels are low, I see no need to repeat testing before considering treatment. However, if he has absent libido and his total T is 900 ng/dL, I might repeat the test to make sure there has not been a laboratory error.

Q. *My total testosterone values are in the low–normal range, but I have many of the symptoms of low T. My physician refuses to treat me because he says my testosterone values are normal. What can I do?*

A. Give him a copy of this book! Seriously, there is a good chance you have low T and will respond to treatment. Ask your doctor to repeat the test and also to obtain free T and SHBG. If either the total T or free T value comes back low, he may be willing to offer you a trial of treatment. If he still won't consider treatment, you can go online at issam.ch/freetesto.htm and obtain your calculated free T value by submitting your total T and SHBG values. If this is low, you've got a strong case. If he still won't help, find another physician who may be more familiar with testosterone issues and be willing to help you.

Q. *I have a very low testosterone concentration, but my physician says I couldn't really have low T because my LH is within the normal range. Is he right?*

A. This is a common misconception. In training, most of us learned only two possibilities of what could happen when testosterone was low. Either LH would be high, indicating testicular failure, or LH would be low, indicating a pituitary or hypothalamus problem. Over the last twenty years, we have learned that the most common cause of low T is aging; in most of these cases, LH will be within the normal range. LH has little importance except for giving us clues as to why testosterone may be low. If you have low T, you have low T, regardless of what the LH shows.

Q. *Do I need to fast before I have my blood test for testosterone?*

A. No.

Q. *If I have sex on the morning when I have my blood test, will that affect the result?*

A. No.

Q. *Is it possible to have low T despite having a deep voice?*

A. Yes. And it is a myth that being injured in the testicles (or even losing them!) will produce a high-pitched voice. Once the larynx, or voicebox, has enlarged during puberty under the influence of testosterone, it will not become smaller again even if T levels are greatly reduced.

Q. *I've read that low T is a myth promoted by the pharmaceutical companies so that they can sell more testosterone. Is that true?*

A. No. The effects of low T have been recognized in men for centuries, long before there were any pharmaceutical companies and before anyone knew the word *testosterone*.

Chapter 5

Benefits of Testosterone Therapy

So far, we have covered the symptoms of low testosterone, and I've shared stories from my patients to illustrate many of the ways that testosterone therapy has relieved their symptoms and improved their lives. In this chapter, I will provide more details regarding the specific actions of T therapy on the body and review several of the key studies that demonstrate the effect of T therapy on sexual function, mood, muscles, and other areas.

Sexual Benefits of T Therapy

How good is testosterone therapy for treatment of sexual symptoms in men with low T? Pretty darn good, although it is important to understand that sex is complicated. (But then, you knew that, right?) There are a number of different aspects of sex, such as erections, desire, orgasm, or sensitivity, that may be affected by low T or by other physical conditions, although not all of them may respond to the same extent just by normalizing T levels in the blood. In addition, there can be social or psychological factors that influence sexual desire and sexual performance. There is no way that T therapy can heal a failing marriage or any number of other personal circumstances that may be adversely affecting a sexual relationship. Nonetheless, T therapy is often just the ticket when sexual symptoms are caused by low T.

Increased Libido

The hallmark symptom of low T is reduced libido. Libido refers to the inner hunger, the drive, to have sex. Sometimes men are confused when I ask about their sexual desire. One man in his midforties said to me, "Doctor, of course I want to have sex with my wife—she's a beautiful thirty-eight-year-old woman, and if I don't have sex with her, she's going to go somewhere else for it." This answer had to do with recognition of the importance of sex in a relationship, but had nothing to do with the inner hunger for sex that we usually refer to as sex drive, or libido.

In one study, my colleagues and I asked 211 men with low T how T therapy had affected them. The average age of these men was fifty-five years, with a range of thirty to seventy-nine years. Almost two-thirds of them experienced an increase in their libido with T therapy, and this response rate was similar for all age groups. Men with T concentrations between 200 and 300 ng/dL had the greatest response rate, with a slightly lower benefit seen in men whose T concentrations were above or below this range.

This improvement in libido with T therapy appears to be well maintained for years among those who respond. In a study by Dr. Christina Wang and colleagues at UCLA, men were followed for three and a half years after beginning testosterone therapy, making it the longest study of this type for testosterone treatment. A substantial improvement in libido was noted at the earliest follow-up and was maintained at the same level for the duration of the study. This means that T therapy does more than offer a short-term boost to a man's sex drive. What really happens, for those who respond to treatment, is that the restoration of adequate testosterone concentrations in the bloodstream allows a man to feel what he would consider a normal—or at least improved—sex drive for as long as his testosterone levels are all right. In my practice, we counsel men that they may see improvement in as little as several weeks, but that it may take one to two months for them to notice a difference.

Because testosterone has been so closely tied to libido, it is often asked why the response rate isn't 100 percent with T therapy. The answer is that libido, as well as other aspects of sexuality, is the result of biological and psychological processes that involve much more than just testosterone concentrations. In fact, it is worthwhile to recognize that for both men and women there can be significant intervals of time when sexual interest fades for a while, even among individuals with completely normal hormone levels. Stress can certainly play a role in this. Even among laboratory animals, conditions of high stress can eliminate the willingness of males to mate with available females (and vice versa).

Reduced Erectile Dysfunction (ED)

Erectile dysfunction is like a power failure for the penis. The man may be fully aroused, but his penis just doesn't respond. With the saturation marketing of the oral medications Viagra, Cialis, and Levitra, it is easy to conclude that these medications can solve every man's ED problem. Unfortunately, this is not the case. And even if it were, these pills may not be the best solution for a man with ED.

Until quite recently, the prevailing wisdom was that testosterone replacement therapy (TRT) was not particularly helpful for the treatment of ED. During my medical training in the 1980s, we were taught that only 5 percent of men with ED responded well to T therapy. Several studies performed over the last ten years have shown this to be incorrect. Not only can T therapy help with ED, but it can even help men who have failed full-dose treatment with Viagra.

As discussed in Chapter 2, testosterone has important actions on the brain as well as on the vascular structures of the penis, so it is a critical component of erections. It should not be surprising, then, that low T can affect a man's sexual performance and that T therapy can be an effective form of treatment for ED.

In the same study of 211 men who received T therapy, approximately 60 percent of them reported improvement in erections. Again, age did not affect response rates, but the group most likely to note improvement in erections were those with the mildest T deficiency (T > 300 ng/dL).

One study from Italy took a group of twenty men with low T, all of whom had poor arterial function as the basis for their ED and all of whom had failed treatment with 100 mg of Viagra. They then were started on treatment with either a testosterone patch or a placebo patch. After one month, the men on T therapy were found to have increased arterial flow in the penis, and they reported improved erections. The men on placebo were unchanged. This study demonstrates the important effects of testosterone on the blood vessels of the penis.

Another study looked at the ability of T therapy to help men who had failed full-dose treatment with sildenafil (Viagra). Thirty-two of these men, all with low T, underwent T therapy. For the first two months, they attempted to have intercourse without any other medications apart from testosterone. If unsuccessful, they were then allowed to also use sildenafil. At the end of the study, one-third of the men reported adequate erections for intercourse with T therapy alone, another third achieved success with the combination of T therapy and Viagra, and the last third was still unsuccessful. Not only can T therapy improve erections by itself, but in many cases T therapy can "rescue" the response to Viagra or to the other pills, Cialis and Levitra. Normal levels of testosterone allow the ED pills to work their magic.

This brings up an important question: What is the best way to treat a man with ED if he also happens to have low T? The oral medications for ED are a great solution for men with a vascular basis for their ED or those who have a "shy penis" due to performance anxiety. However, men with low testosterone tend to also have other symptoms in addition to ED. Indeed, whether or not they recognize it, the ED may have resulted from a lack of sex drive. After all, if a man is less than fully aroused, then it would be understandable if he were unable to achieve a full erection.

Another benefit of T therapy is that when it works, the man is made whole again. He no longer needs to take a pill in anticipation of having sex. One of the most common complaints about the oral medications is that men feel like they are on a stopwatch or under pressure to actually have sex soon after taking the pill. Perhaps most important, there is the psychological piece to the puzzle. Men with ED who respond well to the pills still often describe themselves as "impotent," whereas men whose sex lives have been restored due to T therapy usually say they feel normal again.

For these reasons, for a man with low T, I will almost always begin treatment with T therapy. If the man continues to have no sexual success after a couple of months, I then will prescribe one of the oral ED medications.

Nonsexual Benefits of T Therapy

With increasing awareness of the symptoms of low T, more and more men are interested in learning whether T therapy might benefit them in ways that have nothing to do with sex. One of the more fascinating areas of current investigation is the effect of T therapy on body composition and function, including effects on muscle and fat and on risk factors for heart disease. Below, I describe some of the more important findings in this area.

Improved Body Composition

One of testosterone's most reliable effects is the way it impacts body composition. On the whole, men who begin T therapy will find an increase in their overall body weight, but not because they are getting fatter. On the contrary, the rise in body weight is due to an increase in muscle, referred to as lean body mass in medical terminology. This increased body weight occurs even though the amount of fat in the body is decreased by T therapy.

In the three-and-a-half-year study of testosterone gel by Dr. Wang and colleagues, the average weight of men increased by 1.2 kg or about 2.5 lb. This change in weight was noted at six months and did not change much throughout the remaining three years of the study. This makes sense, because it is the change in testosterone that precipitates the changes in muscle and fat. Once a new level is established, it appears that no major additional changes will occur—unless, of course, a man decides to go on a diet or a fitness kick, which will change any man's weight, regardless of his T status.

More Muscle

Muscle is one of the key areas of testosterone action. Particularly recently, with the various steroid scandals among athletes, it seems we read about the effects of testosterone on muscle in the newspapers every day. To a great extent, the stories about testosterone and muscles are true. More testosterone leads to more muscle bulk and strength, especially at the super-high levels used by athletes and bodybuilders, and less testosterone leads to loss of muscle bulk and strength.

One of the more interesting recent observations is that testosterone actually seems able to create more muscle cells. When I was in medical school, I was taught that the number of cells in any adult muscle was constant over the course of adult life. Exercise might bulk up that muscle, but only by making each muscle cell larger and stronger. Well, that concept has turned out to be incorrect. Not only do higher testosterone levels help with the strength and size of each individual muscle cell, but testosterone also influences nearby cells into becoming muscle cells. This process is called recruitment. More muscle cells leads to greater strength and size.

Although it is common for multiple studies of a subject to come to different conclusions, studies in this field all come to a consistent result: T therapy increases the amount of muscle in the body. In the three-and-a-half-year study of T gel mentioned earlier, the amount of muscle added was 4.4 lb at six months, increasing to 6.3 lb at eighteen months. That's a lot of new muscle!

The effect of testosterone on muscle has been studied under a variety of conditions. One common finding is that testosterone administration results in an increase in strength that is roughly equal to the increase seen with exercise alone. As a rule, the combination of T administration plus exercise leads to the best results. In one study of forty-seven men, T therapy alone led to a 17 percent increase in the maximum amount of weight used in a leg press. Resistance training alone resulted in a similar 17 percent increase, but the combination of T therapy and resistance training provided an increase of 27 percent.

Curiously, it appears that T therapy helps some muscles more than others when it comes to strength. In most studies that measured leg strength, T therapy had a significant effect. However, arm or grip strength improved in some T studies but not in others.

The reason for this disparity between T therapy's effect on upper and lower body strength is not well understood.

The reason athletes and bodybuilders take such high dosages of testosterone and related body-enhancing medications is that the effect on muscle appears to be related to dosage. Dosages that bring testosterone above the normal range appear to have a greater effect on muscle bulk and strength than normal doses. However, the health risks of raising testosterone so much higher than normal levels are unknown. The medical goals of T therapy are to increase T concentration into the normal range, not above it, and I fully support this objective.

Reduced Fat

One of the less well-known effects of T therapy is its effects on body fat. For reasons that are only beginning to be understood, testosterone not only increases muscle in the body, but also reduces fat.

In the study by Dr. Wang and colleagues, men receiving T therapy lost 1.75 lb of fat in the first six months, and dropped a total of 3 lb of fat by 18 months. In another study that looked at the details of T's effect on adipose (fat) tissue, fifty-four healthy young men ages eighteen to thirty-five years underwent treatment that suppressed their own testosterone secretion and were then administered various doses of testosterone injections, creating several groups with average T levels ranging from lower than normal to much higher than normal. Participants placed on low doses of testosterone developed increased amounts of fat below the skin, inside the abdomen, and between muscles. Those placed on high doses had reductions in the amount of fat between the muscles, without changes in other areas.

Although T therapy cannot compare to the tried-and-true weight-loss programs that usually involve diet and exercise, many men do appreciate the changes in body composition that accompany T therapy.

Increased Bone Density

Over the last decade or two, we have learned that testosterone is also important for bone health. Men whose T levels have been reduced to extremely low concentrations as part of therapy for prostate cancer have reduced bone density and are at increased risk of fractures. Recently, it was shown that men with naturally occurring low concentrations of testosterone may also be at increased risk of fractures.

In an important paper published in 2008, researchers followed 609 men older than sixty years of age living in Dubbo, Australia, for up to thirteen years. During this time, 113 of these men suffered at least one bone fracture resulting from relatively minor injuries. There was no difference in the fracture rate between men with medium T concentrations and men with high T concentrations, but men with low T had double the risk of fracture as the rest of the study population. This is the first solid evidence indicating that not only does low T contribute to lower bone density, but also that this reduction in bone density leads to an increased risk of fractures from relatively minor injuries.

T therapy significantly improves bone density at the hip and spine (the usual locations where bone density is measured). This has been demonstrated in nearly all studies involving T administration, as long as the men receiving testosterone actually had low T to begin with. The results have not been as reliable when T levels have been fairly normal. This makes sense, because the evidence suggests that normal T levels are probably adequate for optimal bone density.

It is important to note that it may take a long time to see the changes in bone density with T therapy—or with any other therapy, for that matter. In one study, the improvement at the hip didn't show up until the third year of treatment. Improvement at the spine occurred more quickly, but it still took more than a year. For this reason, bone density measurements are usually obtained no more frequently than at yearly intervals.

Better General Health

What does it mean to be healthy? In the most general sense, we tend to mean that someone seems fit and does not have major risk factors for serious illness. Although it may not always be specified, those risk factors are usually about two things: cardiovascular disease (heart attacks and strokes being the most important) and cancer. New research suggests that testosterone may play an important role in both of these areas. In this section, I describe some of the important studies regarding testosterone and cardiovascular disease, leaving the relationship of testosterone and prostate cancer to Chapter 7.

There are several key, interrelated factors involved in cardiovascular health, and testosterone appears to play an important role in many of them. These factors include obesity, high blood sugar, hypertension, and lipids, including cholesterol. Each of these factors alone represents a risk for cardiovascular disease. But the presence of several of these factors raises the risk considerably and is called the metabolic syndrome. Testosterone is associated not only with the metabolic syndrome overall, but also with several of the individual components.

For example, men with a waist circumference of more than 40 inches have been shown to have lower T levels than men with smaller waist circumferences, and this is an important measure of obesity. Low T has also been associated with a more commonly known indicator of obesity called BMI (for body mass index), which is calculated using one's height and weight. Men with a high BMI—which is a risk factor for cardiovascular disease—are more likely to have low T.

The story of blood sugar and its relationship to testosterone is even more impressive. When blood sugar is very elevated, the condition is called diabetes. Men with diabetes are at increased risk for a number of health problems, especially cardiovascular disease. In one study, 110 men with diabetes were compared to 875 men without diabetes. Among men with diabetes, 21 percent had a total T less than 350 ng/dL, compared with 13 percent of nondiabetic men. Overall, men with diabetes had lower T levels than nondiabetic men, even after adjustment for BMI.

In another study of diabetic men who happened to also have a high average BMI, 41 percent were found to have low T. Even more interesting with regard to the relationship between testosterone and blood sugar regulation, the presence of low T increased the risk of developing diabetes later in life by approximately 50 percent.

One of the best known risk factors for cardiovascular disease is having a high concentration of cholesterol in the bloodstream. Over the years, we have learned that there are subtypes of cholesterol to which we also need to pay attention, so we now routinely measure high-density lipoprotein (HDL), known as "good" cholesterol because it appears to be protective against atherosclerosis and heart disease, and low-density lipoprotein (LDL), known as "bad" cholesterol because high levels are associated with increased risk of disease. Although it was once feared that T therapy might worsen cholesterol values, several recent studies have shown that T therapy can decrease both total cholesterol as well as LDL, the bad cholesterol.

In one study, twenty-four men underwent treatment with either T injections or placebo injections for three months, followed by a one-month "washout period" where they received no treatment, and then each man was switched to the other treatment for the next three months. The results of the study showed that when men were on T injections, there was a reduction in fasting blood sugar, waist circumference, and total cholesterol.

Healthier Heart

Not only does testosterone appear to influence risk factors for cardiovascular disease, but there is also evidence that it may play a direct beneficial role for the heart itself. One key observation in multiple studies is that men with coronary artery disease appear to have lower T levels than men without coronary artery disease.

There also appear to be beneficial effects of T therapy for men once heart disease has already developed. A study of fifty men with low T and known heart disease randomized the group into weekly testosterone injections or injections of a placebo. At the end of eight weeks, the T injection group had fewer electrocardiogram (EKG) changes during exercise. In contrast, there were no fewer EKG changes in the patients taking the placebo. Another study of sixty-two men with known heart disease treated half the participants first with T therapy for a month and the other half with a placebo for a month, followed by two weeks without any treatment for either group. Then each group switched over to the other treatment for another month. During the monthlong periods of T therapy, men experienced less chest pain and fewer EKG changes than they did during the monthlong periods of placebo treatment.

The small number of studies in humans support the idea that T therapy may be beneficial for men with heart disease, but there is clearly more work to be done in this area.

What Do All These Studies Mean?

The point of sharing all these various studies is to show that T therapy has important effects on many parts of our bodies. Restoring T to normal levels provides a host of health benefits: more muscle, less fat, stronger bones, and even likely benefits to the heart. This sounds like pie-in-the-sky stuff. Can testosterone really be that good?

The answer is a qualified yes. The effects are real, but it is important to put them all in perspective. These studies all looked at results for groups of men rather than individuals. And the reason studies tend to ignore individual results is that one person may respond very differently from another. Group effects tend to be more reliable than individual ones. For this reason, no one can promise that any one individual will see all—or any—of the benefits of T therapy that I've outlined here. In other words, most men will lose some fat with T therapy, to take but one example, but some men might not.

Another thing to realize is that the magnitude of the effect will vary from individual to individual. Some men may noticeably gain muscle bulk and strength, whereas others may add only a little bit. Even more important, it should be made perfectly clear that by restoring testosterone to normal levels rather than to the crazy-high levels of athletes hoping to enhance their athletic performance, we are unlikely to cause any drastic transformation of anyone's body composition. The changes with T therapy are real, but it's not as if an old friend won't recognize you anymore after you've been on T therapy for a while.

There are other areas of investigation into T therapy that I have not reviewed in this chapter but have mentioned along the way—areas such as effects on brain function, energy, sense of vigor and vitality, and other sexual symptoms as well. Some of these areas have simply not been adequately studied, while for others it has been a challenge to even find the right questions to ask in a study. For example, exactly how would one define a sense of vigor? Many individuals would use the old legal definition of pornography: "I don't know how to define it, but I sure know how to recognize it when I see it." Or, in this case, *feel* it. But this fuzziness about how to define feelings like a sense of vigor make it exceedingly challenging to study. Thus, in this chapter, I've only focused on several of the best-studied aspects of T therapy's effects on the body.

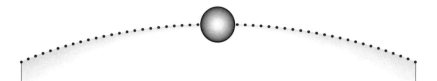

Questions and Answers

Q. *When I joined my athletic club, one of the first things they did was measure my percentage of body fat. Would T therapy reduce this percentage?*

A. Probably. T therapy increases the amount of lean body mass, which is basically muscle, and decreases fat mass. This should decrease the percentage of your body that is composed of fat. Exercise does the same thing, and the combination of normal T together with exercise produces the best results.

Q. *I have painful tennis elbow. Could this be a symptom of osteoporosis?*

A. No. The only symptom of osteoporosis is fracturing a bone from a relatively minor injury. In other words, there are no symptoms until it's too late. To find out if someone has osteoporosis requires a simple, noninvasive test that measures the density of the bones.

Q. *I'm healthy, but there's a lot of heart disease in my family. Should I start T therapy to prevent a heart attack?*

A. Unfortunately, there is no evidence that T therapy will prevent heart attacks or that it is indicated to treat heart disease. The evidence that higher levels of testosterone appear to be beneficial for the heart is promising, but too new for any recommendations of this type. On the other hand, if you have any symptoms of low T, you might wish to begin T therapy to treat those symptoms. Perhaps your heart might benefit, too.

Q. *I'm sixty years old and an avid golfer. When I was fifty, I could drive the ball 250 yards without even trying. Now I'm lucky if I can put it out there 200 yards. My doctor diagnosed me with low T, and I do have some of the other usual symptoms. But what I'm really curious about is whether T therapy will improve my distance off the tee? Would it be considered cheating?*

A. It's quite possible that T therapy might help your golf game. I have quite a few patients whose only symptom of low T was reduced athletic performance and who were very pleased with the results of T therapy. Some of them also felt better in ways they hadn't expected. As for cheating, it's important to recognize that the goal of T therapy is only to restore T levels to normal, to levels that probably match your own natural T concentrations from ten to twenty years ago. My opinion is that this is not cheating as long as T levels are maintained in the normal range—it's just allowing an individual to reach the potential he would have with normal hormone levels.

Q. *If T therapy helps muscle strength as much as exercise does, then what's the point of exercise? What's to stop me from just taking T therapy and hanging out on the couch watching TV and improving my body that way?*

A. You're right—the evidence shows that on average, men with low T do get as much muscle benefit from T therapy alone as they do from exercise alone. But they do much better if they exercise once their T levels have been restored to normal. The choice is yours, of course, but the benefits of exercise go way beyond muscle strength and mass, including building up your cardiovascular capability. T therapy alone won't get your heart rate up or make you sweat. I'm afraid that becoming truly fit still requires time and effort!

Chapter 6

Treatment for Low Testosterone Levels

When testosterone therapy was first developed more than sixty years ago, the only form of treatment was a daily injection. Fortunately, we now have a much wider and more convenient set of treatment modalities, including patches, gels, and even a pellet that is placed above the gumline in the mouth. Testosterone injections have improved as well, with injections lasting two to three weeks. An exciting alternative is placement of extended-release pellets below the skin that provide normal T levels for three to six months, requiring only a few visits per year.

The variety of treatment options leads to a number of questions. Which one is best for me? What are the advantages of one over another? Are there greater risks or disadvantages to some? In this chapter, I will review these various options and address these questions.

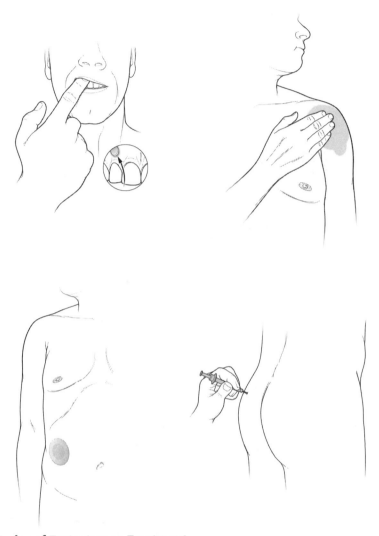

Modes of Testosterone Treatment

Testosterone treatments are available in several forms. Upper left, buccal treatment consists of a pellet that adheres high on the gums, above the teeth. Upper right, testosterone gels are applied daily to the upper arms, shoulder, and chest. Bottom left, testosterone patches are usually applied daily to the flank or lower abdomen. Bottom right, injection into the buttock. Use of oral forms (pills) of testosterone (not shown) available in the United States are strongly discouraged due to liver toxicity. Injection of slow-release testosterone pellets (not shown) are also available.

Injections

The first form of T therapy was an intramuscular injection, usually given in the buttocks. In the 1940s, this was a daily treatment with a short-acting form of testosterone called testosterone propionate. Later, a depot formulation was developed that provided a longer duration of action. These longer-acting injectables have two forms of testosterone that can be prescribed—one is testosterone cypionate and the other is testosterone enanthate. They are equivalent and can be used interchangeably.

When I started treating men with testosterone in the late 1980s, the common interval between injections was three to four weeks, and at first I used the same time period between injections. It wasn't long, though, until my patients taught me that an injection every three to four weeks was less than ideal. Many of my patients complained that for a week or more prior to the next injection they experienced a return of their original symptoms. This was because injections in most men raise testosterone for only twelve to fourteen days, after which the level falls back to its baseline. Patients would report back to me about their treatment by saying, "Doctor, I feel great for the first week or two, but then I feel like I was never even treated until I get my next shot." This up-and-down experience with T injections is called the roller-coaster effect.

For the most part, I have prescribed T injections every two weeks. Some men choose to have their injections every seven to ten days to avoid the roller-coaster effect, in which case we teach them to inject themselves. Only an occasional patient chooses to have his injections on a less frequent schedule, usually every three weeks. I strongly discourage the monthly injection of depot testosterone, something that had been quite common in the past, because it results in low levels of testosterone for half of the month.

The only practical disadvantage to more frequent injections is that it can be a literal pain in the butt (sorry, bad urology joke!). Actually, although the usual location for the injection is in the buttock, we teach a lot of men to inject themselves, usually in the thigh. This isn't for everyone, but it is easy to do and not particularly painful. And it frees the men from frequent visits to the office. Of course, men on a less-frequent injection schedule can also learn to self-inject.

There are two main advantages to injections over the other treatments. The first is that if one really wants to know whether raising testosterone levels will improve symptoms, there is no mode of therapy better than injections. Gels or patches may be more convenient, but they often require dose adjustment to achieve optimal levels, and as many as 20 percent of patients never absorb enough to determine whether the symptoms were due to low T. I have had quite a few men respond to injections when they noticed no benefits from T gels or patches. This is almost certainly due to the higher blood concentrations achieved with injections.

The second advantage of injections is cost. On average, the cost for the injectable medication is approximately $5 per treatment. Based on the most recently available prescription data (2005), injections account for approximately 25 percent of T prescriptions. The newer forms of testosterone are usually considerably more expensive and are not always covered by health insurance plans.

Injection Dosage

The standard dose for T injections works out to be 100 mg per week. This means that if someone is on a two-week cycle, each injection will be 200 mg. Depending on response to treatment and the way each body handles medicine differently, some men will need higher doses. It is not uncommon for me to adjust dosage up to 250, 300, and on rare occasions even 400 mg every two weeks.

The reason to increase dosage is that many men will not respond to treatment until their T levels are in the upper range of normal. If normal is something like 350–1,000 ng/dL, this means that some men will need to get above 600–650 ng/dL before they start feeling better.

Because injections provide a rapid rise in T concentrations within the first one to three days, followed by a gradual decline, T levels in these men represent a moving target. T concentrations will almost always be above 1,000 ng/dL for the first few days, then decline into the normal range. I avoid having blood tests obtained soon after injections, because the results are meaningless, and it can be distressing to have levels that appear too high (many an uninitiated physician will have a ministroke thinking that these levels represent a constant high value and will tell their patients to discontinue treatment immediately!). The best times to obtain blood tests are midcycle (e.g., after seven days in a fourteen-day cycle), with the goal being to have blood concentrations somewhere in the 400–600 ng/dL range, or just prior to the next injection, when levels should be in the low–normal range or slightly below. The advantage of checking just prior to the next injection is that the blood test can be done on the same day as the doctor's visit.

The next big thing in testosterone treatment may turn out to be a long-acting injection that is currently under review by the FDA called Nebido. A single injection provides good T levels for ten weeks. This means that a man would only need to show up at the doctor's office five times a year to be treated for low T and would not require any additional treatments. Although Nebido is not yet available in the United States, it has been shown to be safe and effective and has already been in use for several years in many other countries. Because of its convenience, this long-acting injectable form of testosterone will be appealing to many men.

Patches

The first real advance over injections was the T patch. With the patch, men were freed from frequent visits to the doctor's office and from repeated injections. In addition to these practical considerations, the patch also offered more uniform T concentrations, eliminating the roller-coaster effect that frequently occurs with injections.

Several problems with patches limit their usefulness. One is that T levels tend to only reach into the lower range of normal, and in some men the absorption may be too poor to achieve a beneficial response at all. Another is the awkwardness of having a visible patch on the body, which can be awkward for men who undress at the gym or for men who perhaps are dating and not yet ready to share their medical issues with a sexual partner. A major limitation is that patches cause skin irritation in as many as 44 percent of men in one study, with wearers experiencing bright red, round blotches at the location of the patch for a few days after it had been removed.

Nonetheless, patches can be quite useful and today make up approximately 12 percent of the testosterone market. I have quite a few patients who had started treatment with patches when they first came on the market and have been happy with this form of treatment for fifteen years. For the most part, however, the patch has been supplanted by the T gels, which offer greater efficacy and convenience. The one specific situation where I recommend a trial of T patches is for the man who wishes to avoid injections and who dislikes applying a gel to his skin. For some men, application of the patch, Androderm, is simpler and less messy than gels and thus is more appealing.

Gels

Testosterone gels are the most common form of treatment in the United States, accounting for 60 percent of the testosterone market. There are two FDA-approved formulations, AndroGel and Testim. Once a day, the man applies the prescribed amount of gel to his skin and rubs it in. The recommended areas are the upper arms and shoulders. Bathing and showering should not occur for the first two hours after application, because much of the gel will be washed away. Skin irritation is rare. The advantages of the gel are that nothing is visible and there are no red blotches, no injections, and no need for frequent doctor's visits.

The other major advantage of the gels is that their absorption is much better than the patches. Some men absorb the medication so effectively that the standard starting dose of 5 g causes T levels to exceed 1,000, and the dose has to be reduced. However, there is great variability in absorption from one individual to another, and early blood tests are necessary to evaluate and adjust dosages to achieve a good testosterone concentration. As with the patch, the gel should be applied daily. After twenty-four hours, testosterone concentrations usually drop close to baseline levels, so skipping a day means that T levels will be suboptimal. Although absorption tends to be excellent, approximately 15–20 percent of men simply do not absorb the gel well or even at all. For this reason, it is imperative to check blood levels some time after beginning treatment to make sure that treatment is really causing increased T levels in the blood.

Quite a few men have come to me for a second opinion, saying that T therapy hasn't worked for them. The explanation was that they simply hadn't absorbed the gel adequately. A common error is failing to check blood levels for testosterone after prescribing T gel, assuming incorrectly that T levels must be improved just because a man rubs the medication into his skin. Unfortunately, this is not the case. Some men need a higher dose (more gel) than the usual starting amount of 5 g. And some will still fail to absorb properly at a higher dose of 7.5 or 10 g. If this happens, switching brands of T gel is often effective in achieving better absorption. Otherwise, men who fail to absorb gel adequately should try another form of T therapy, usually injections.

AndroGel was the first T gel to come to market. It is clear and odorless and comes in a little foil packet. A newer way of providing the gel is with a pump, which acts like a soap dispenser. The usual starting dose is 5 g, which corresponds to one packet or four pumps. If this dosage fails to provide an adequate T concentration in the blood, the dose can be increased up to 10 g, which corresponds to two packets or eight pumps.

The second gel product is Testim, which comes in a small tube with a cap. The usual dose is one tube daily, which is 5 g, but the dose can be increased to two tubes, or 10 g. There is some evidence that some men may absorb Testim better than AndroGel. However, Testim has an odor or, as the company prefers to say, a "fragrance." This fragrance can be a double-edged sword: some women like the scent of the man's "new cologne," whereas others find it objectionable. A person's response to a fragrance is highly personal, and occasionally I will receive a request for a different gel or mode of treatment because of this.

Gels are easy to use and work well in most men. One issue that limits their use is cost. In some states, such as Massachusetts, T gels are covered by most health insurers and the co-pay is acceptable. But without health insurance coverage, the cost can be as much as $200–$500 per month. If cost is an issue, the best option may be injections or, in some cases, pellets.

Gel Dosage

The usual starting dose for both gels is 5 g. If a man does not achieve good T concentrations with a dose of 5 g, I usually increase the dose to 10 g, but sometimes a smaller increase to 7.5 g is enough. I do not prescribe doses greater than 10 g for a practical reason—the man runs out of skin surface to rub it in! If 10 g doesn't yield adequate T concentrations in the blood, the usual next step is to try injections.

I monitor both total and free T in men receiving T therapy. T therapy will increase both values, but just as with diagnosis, free T results can sometimes be more important than the total T, particularly if the two test results are not in close agreement. In general, I aim to increase both total and free T into the mid- to upper range of normal to give my patients the best chance of seeing improvement.

Gel Concerns

One concern specific to gels is that some of the testosterone on the surface of the skin can be transferred to others who come in contact with the man's skin. Because women and children have very low levels of testosterone compared to men, the fear is that if they absorb some of the testosterone from the man, higher T levels will make a woman appear more hairy or masculine or may cause similar kinds of problems for little boys and girls.

This is not a very significant concern. In one study, men and women were instructed to rub against each other vigorously for fifteen minutes after the man applied gel. Blood tests in the women did show an increase in testosterone, but it was mild. And even if T levels did rise substantially, this shouldn't be a problem if the exposure happened infrequently. However, repeated, frequent exposures of this type have been reported to cause changes in women and children, and it makes sense to take precautions against this.

Practically speaking, the T gel is on the surface of the skin for only one to two hours. So I instruct my patients that if they intend to get "frisky" within the first two hours after applying the gel, they should either shower first or throw on a T shirt to cover the application areas. I have never had a patient report to me any changes in their partners or children that could be attributed to absorption of testosterone.

For similar reasons, it is recommended that men avoid swimming and showering for the first two hours after gel application, because these activities will wash away the gel and they will not get a full dose. Once again, after a couple hours there is likely to be no impact on the concentration of gel, because nearly all of it has been absorbed inside the surface of the skin.

Compounded Testosterone Creams

Some pharmacies advertise their ability to make, or compound, their own testosterone creams. They take testosterone, mix it with the materials used to create creams, and sell it in competition with AndroGel and Testim. These compounded T creams seem to be particularly appealing to men and their physicians who are interested in antiaging medicine and dietary and herbal supplements.

When I first started seeing patients in the office who were using these locally compounded testosterone creams, I was strongly against them because there was no oversight process such as occurs with the FDA with brand-name medications. When I checked blood tests on these men, however, I soon discovered that many of them did have reasonable T levels. These days, if a man comes to see me with good T levels while using a compounded T product, I will not automatically switch him to a brand-name gel, as I once did.

But I would not choose such a cream to begin treatment. Let's be clear: one of the most important benefits of medications passing through the approval process of the FDA is that pharmaceutical companies are required to prove that the medication does what it is supposed to do, that there is consistency in its manufacturing, and that the amount of medicine should be the same from one batch to the next, whether the prescription is filled in Kansas City or in Tampa. There is no way that a local pharmacy can do this. So, unless there is a good reason provided by my patient to do otherwise, I always prescribe the FDA-approved formulations.

Testosterone Pellets

An appealing treatment choice is the use of extended-release pellets that are inserted under the skin, usually in the buttock. This product is called Testopel. The advantage of these pellets is that they maintain good levels of testosterone for three to six months, so patients don't need to apply gel every day or receive injections every couple of weeks. These pellets are each about the size of a grain of rice, and six to eight of them usually are inserted at a time. Insertion is painlessly performed in the office with local anesthesia and requires only a few minutes.

Pellets are both a new yet old treatment in that they were first approved by the FDA many years ago, but most physicians knew little about them. However, physicians and patients alike have recently become aware of the benefits of a longer-acting testosterone treatment, leading to new interest in pellets. I find that many of my patients prefer the idea of pellet insertion a few times a year over an injection every two weeks. And some men are relieved to have a simpler morning routine that does not require several minutes of rubbing gel into their skin.

Buccal Treatment

One of the more inventive treatments for low T is a pellet applied to the gums above the teeth. This is called the buccal mode of treatment, and the name of the product is Striant. This pellet has an adhesive that sticks to the gum, and the pellet stays there all day, allowing testosterone to be absorbed via the gums, but not permitting testosterone to seep out into the mouth or into saliva. Studies have confirmed there is no danger of transferring testosterone to others by kissing or sharing food. The pellet is replaced every twelve hours, in the morning and then again in the evening.

Only a small number of my patients use this form of treatment, but the ones who do are quite pleased. Their testosterone levels have been good, and these men tell me that after a few days they are not even aware that the pellet is present. They have not experienced any gum irritation or other unpleasantness, and it is not visible with smiling or talking. To see it, the upper lip must be lifted way up, so there is little danger of someone asking why they have something stuck above their teeth. And although my patients have not complained of the pellet becoming dislodged during eating, chewing gum is discouraged.

The buccal treatment will never be a leading form of treatment, but it should be considered in men who have sensitive skin or who dislike applying gels or creams.

Pills

Testosterone does come in pills, but this form of treatment is associated with a significant risk of liver toxicity. For this reason, the use of pills for the treatment of low T is strongly discouraged. Instead, these testosterone pills have been used to treat a small number of rare disorders, where the severity of the illness justifies the risk of treatment. One example is men whose bone marrow has stopped making red blood cells properly.

Fortunately, the standard forms of treatment for low T—injections, patches, gels, buccal pellets—do not share this liver toxicity. In addition, there is one form of oral testosterone that does not cause liver trouble, but it is not available in the United States. It is called testosterone undecanoate and goes by the trade name Andriol. The company that manufactures Andriol has no apparent intention of bringing this medication to the United States, which is too bad, because my Canadian colleagues who have prescribed it think that it is a useful and effective therapy. However, it does require several doses each day, and blood concentrations of testosterone may not always reach optimal levels with this treatment.

Clomiphene Citrate and Anastrozole

Although oral forms of testosterone in the United States are almost never used to treat low T, there are two types of pills that can still be useful. These pills are not testosterone itself, but instead are medications that stimulate the body to produce more of its own testosterone. The pills that I use, clomiphene citrate and anastrozole, fool the body's negative feedback system, and cause an increase in the pituitary's release of luteinizing hormone (LH), which in turn stimulates the testicles to make more testosterone. The beauty of this is that the rise in testosterone comes entirely from increased production by the man's body itself. In concept, this is the most natural form of treatment.

The rationale for this treatment came from experience with men with infertility and reduced numbers of sperm. Trials of clomiphene citrate in the 1980s and later were shown to help sperm counts and fertility in a subset of men. During these studies, it was noted that LH and testosterone levels increased as well.

When I treat men for fertility issues, I always check testosterone levels because testosterone is a critical component of sperm production and maturation and low T can thus contribute to male infertility. Because giving testosterone itself to the body shuts down or greatly reduces LH levels, T production within the testicles is also greatly reduced. In contrast, treatment with clomiphene citrate or anastrozole (which works in similar fashion) increases blood levels of testosterone without reducing sperm counts.

These oral medications improve testosterone levels fairly reliably in younger men and often in older men, too. Curiously, though, some men may develop excellent T levels but notice no improvement in their symptoms. Yet when these men are switched to other forms of testosterone, such as gels, their symptoms respond well. It seems regular testosterone has a more reliably beneficial effect on the brain than these pills, despite good circulatory levels of T.

Human Chorionic Gonadotropin (HCG) Injections

Human chorionic gonadotropin, or HCG, is an infrequently used treatment for low T because it requires frequent injections, usually three times each week. HCG mimics LH, stimulating the Leydig cells in the testicles to produce more T. The primary use of HCG in men is for young individuals with significant hormonal abnormalities, such as those who have failed to properly undergo puberty, and for men with infertility associated with deficiencies of LH and testosterone.

Supplements and Natural Therapies

There is great interest in alternative methods to treat low T. Many individuals have positive associations with dietary interventions, supplements, herbal therapies, vitamins, or similar treatments. In addition, many men wish to avoid prescription medications, preferring instead to take a more natural route, if possible.

As much as I want to support these approaches, there is not a single shred of evidence that these treatments offer any help to men with low T. Instead, some of the manufacturers of supplements have come up with strongly suggestive brand names for mixtures of supplements. One that was promoted heavily on the radio a few years ago was called Testosterall, with claims that it improved hormone levels and helped with all things manly. It consisted of an assortment of herbs and supplements, such as ginseng and horny goat weed, none of which has ever been shown to help with sexual performance or to increase testosterone.

Another supplement promoted as helping men with their sexual performance was analyzed as part of a medical study and was found to contain small amounts of sildenafil, otherwise known as Viagra. This could certainly help a man's performance! The problem is that Viagra can have troublesome interactions with other medications. Purchasing a supplement that secretly contains Viagra or similar prescription medications is not only misleading, but also potentially dangerous.

There are a few things that are important for consumers to know about supplements. One is that the manufacturers are not yet restricted in their ads by the FDA as long as they do not claim to treat any real medical conditions. So they can't say their product treats erectile dysfunction (a real medical diagnosis), for example, but they can certainly say—and they do—that their product will improve sexual performance (no medical diagnosis). No proof is required—which is convenient because none exists.

Another thing to realize is that the reason these agents are not covered by the FDA and do not require prescriptions is because they have little, if any, important effects on significant medical conditions such as low T. If a supplement or vitamin really increased T levels substantially, it would be critical for the FDA to regulate it.

The only agent available over the counter with some plausible claim to affect male hormone levels is dehydroepiandrosterone (DHEA). DHEA is a precursor of testosterone, and most of it comes from the adrenal glands. Although there has been some debate about the potential benefits of DHEA for years, administration of DHEA in men has so far not been shown to have significant effects or to substantially raise T levels.

Exercise

It is certainly understandable that men would like to be able to increase their testosterone naturally. One comment seen routinely in men's magazines is that strenuous exercise, particularly resistance exercise, will increase testosterone levels in men. The evidence for this is a little thin, but there are a few scientific reports that measured testosterone in younger and older men, noticing a difference in serum testosterone levels. Others did not show any difference in testosterone. And nearly all the studies were done in men with normal testosterone levels. It is unknown whether exercise would increase T at all in men with low T. Another drawback is that the magnitude of the change in testosterone was very small even in the studies that suggested exercise was beneficial. And small increases in T are highly unlikely to convert a man from feeling poorly to feeling great again.

The bottom line is that I never discourage anyone from beginning an exercise regimen because there are so many definite benefits that come from doing so. But I do not believe that exercise alone has much chance of increasing blood levels of testosterone to any significant degree, so I do not go out of my way to recommend exercise as a treatment for low T.

Putting It All Together

As you can see from this chapter, there is quite an assortment of treatments available to increase testosterone in men with low T. How does a man choose which one is right for him?

I generally begin T therapy with gels. They are easy to use, good T concentrations are achieved in a large majority of men, the dosage can be adjusted if needed, and men do not complain of the roller-coaster highs and lows sometimes associated with injections. I reserve injections for men who fail to achieve good T concentrations with gels, for men who dislike applying gels, or in cases where insurance doesn't cover the gels (injections are much less costly). I don't prescribe the patch very often anymore for men newly diagnosed with low T, although I still have patients who have been happy with their patch therapy for many years. Occasionally, there has been a man who disliked the feeling of applying the gel, just like there are men who hate applying sunscreen, and a patch may be less objectionable to those men.

Pellets have become a valuable recent addition to my practice. The insertion technique is almost completely painless, and patients like the freedom of not needing a daily treatment or frequent injection. Long-lasting injections may share these same benefits when they are finally approved for use.

Finally, for men who are interested in achieving a pregnancy with their partner within the next year or so, treatment is limited to the oral medications such as clomiphene citrate and the various aromatase inhibitors, or injections of HCG, which are administered three times per week.

Regardless of the mode of therapy, the key is to find a treatment that

1. Produces T levels high enough to provide symptomatic benefit
2. Isn't so bothersome or annoying that a man stops using the treatment

We're fortunate to have several excellent choices of T therapies in the United States. And at the rapid rate that medicine and technology are changing, we're likely to have even more choices within the next five to ten years.

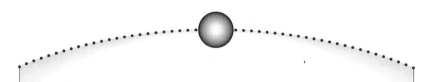

Questions and Answers

Q. *How do I know I'm on the right dose of testosterone gel?*

A. There are two issues to address in determining the right dose of testosterone for men. First, are your symptoms better? Second, have your blood levels of testosterone been optimized? If you feel improvement and your testosterone levels are within the normal range, then you are taking the right dose. If your symptoms are not improved and testosterone levels are not at least in the midrange of normal (e.g., 500 ng/dL), then it is worthwhile to increase the dose and see if symptoms improve. It is always worthwhile to monitor both total and free T levels, particularly if there had been a discrepancy in results for these two tests at the time of diagnosis.

Q. *My original testosterone level was 295 ng/dL when I was first diagnosed with low T, but after one month of treatment with gel my testosterone concentration has declined to 275 ng/dL. Why would testosterone treatment lower my T level?*

A. The levels aren't lower—they are unchanged. The variability in T results is so large that values within 50 ng/dL of each other should be considered the same. Your problem is not that your T levels have decreased, but that they haven't increased. One option is to increase the dosage of your T gel, while another is that it may be worthwhile to try injections for two to three months to see if your symptoms improve.

Q. *I have responded very well to my testosterone gel treatment, and my T levels were within the normal range at my last visit. But after a year, I had my blood checked again and my doctor told me the levels were much too high. He's concerned and wants to stop treatment. What should I do?*

A. You should repeat the blood test, taking care to not apply any gel to the lower arm or inner part of the elbow where blood is usually drawn. One common reason that men will have very high blood test results is that trace amounts of gel can be picked up from the surface of the skin by the needle when blood is obtained. It would be very unusual to have high T concentrations in the blood when previous results on the same dose of medication were normal.

Q. *I've been on testosterone treatment for several years but stopped it when I had surgery two months ago. I've recovered nicely and want to restart treatment. Is it dangerous to start and stop treatment?*

A. There is no evidence that stopping treatment suddenly causes any trouble, nor is there a problem with starting it back up again. Some men who have had good T levels due to treatment will go through a "down" time after discontinuing the medicine that lasts up to a few weeks, but in general their T levels should return to their baseline.

Q. *I'm doing well with T treatment, but I hate the idea of needing to be on this treatment for the rest of my life. For how long will I need it?*

A. T treatment can be stopped anytime. Usually, the original symptoms will return, though, and so most men who respond to treatment continue with it indefinitely. But this should not be regarded as a medical requirement. It is a personal choice for optimizing quality of life.

Q. *Can treatment with testosterone jump-start my body so that I will make more testosterone on my own?*

A. The vast majority of men with low T will continue to have low T if they discontinue treatment. However, I have seen some men develop normal T levels after discontinuing treatment. These men usually had some problem, such as an illness, that affected their body's hormonal regulation. Their T levels returned to normal once they became healthy again.

Chapter 7

Testosterone and Prostate Cancer

Until just a few years ago, it was almost universally believed that T therapy would lead to some degree of increased risk of prostate cancer. During that time T therapy was seen to represent the proverbial pact with the devil, by trading short-term sexual and physical rewards for the ultimate development of a malignant cancer. Fortunately, this belief has been shown to be incorrect, and medical opinion has begun to shift quite dramatically, with good evidence that T therapy is quite safe for the prostate. There is even now a growing concern that *low* T is a risk for prostate cancer rather than high T.

How the original fear about T and prostate cancer came to be is a fantastic story involving Nobel Prize winners, medical breakthroughs, and a critical paradox that took two-thirds of a century to solve. In the end, it is also a cautionary tale of how it may take years—even decades—to correct a medical "truth" once it has been established. I have taken great pleasure in participating in the evolution of attitudes regarding T and prostate cancer, and here I describe how this all took place.

The relationship of testosterone to prostate cancer has under-gone a significant reevaluation, and all recent evidence has rein-forced the position that T therapy is safe for the prostate. I've been fortunate to have participated in the evolution of this idea, which is of critical importance to anyone considering T therapy.

Origins of the Concern

The basis for the fear that T therapy increases the risk of prostate cancer originated with the work of Charles B. Huggins, a urologist at the University of Chicago. Huggins was initially interested in the medical condition called benign enlargement of the prostate, called benign prostatic hyperplasia (BPH), which causes frequent and urgent urination and also can occasionally cause complete obstruction of the urine passageway. Benjamin Franklin was reported to have suffered from BPH and was credited with invent-ing a tube he inserted through the urine channel to relieve the obstruction.

Curiously, dogs are the only species we know of other than humans that naturally develop prostate problems on a regular basis. At the turn of the twentieth century, there were reports that castration was successful in treating some men with severe obstruction from BPH, and Huggins began experimenting on the effects of castration on BPH in dogs. Not only did the dogs' pros-tates shrink after castration, but Huggins made an additional far-reaching observation.

Huggins noticed that the microscopic appearance of prostates of some of these dogs contained areas that were indistinguishable from human prostate cancers. Even more important, after cas-tration, dogs with these cancerous-appearing areas also demon-strated shrinkage of their prostates. Indeed, when their prostates were removed, the dogs had no further evidence of the cancerous-appearing areas.

Huggins and his coworkers then applied his dog results to humans. By this time, it was known that the key effect of castration was to reduce T levels in the bloodstream. He took a group of men who had prostate cancer that had already spread to their bones and lowered their testosterone levels, either by removing the testicles or by administering estrogen. A blood test called acid phosphatase was high in men with metastatic prostate cancer, and Huggins and his coworkers showed that acid phosphatase dropped substantially within days of lowering testosterone. Of even greater consequence for the future of T therapy, Huggins also reported that administration of testosterone injections to men with prostate cancer caused acid phosphatase to rise. Huggins and his coworkers concluded that reducing testosterone levels caused prostate cancer to shrink and raising testosterone levels caused "enhanced growth" of prostate cancer.

This demonstration of the androgen dependence of prostate cancer was incredibly important, because until that time in the early 1940s prostate cancer was untreatable. From that point forward, lowering testosterone by castration or by estrogen became the standard treatment for advanced disease and remains a mainstay of treatment to this day. Because estrogen treatment caused heart attacks and blood clots in some men, and because most men did not care for the idea of having their testicles removed, a new type of medication—LHRH agonists—was introduced in the 1980s. Injections of this medication are now the usual way testosterone is lowered in men with prostate cancer.

Huggins was eventually awarded the Nobel Prize in 1966 for his work showing that prostate cancer grew or shrank depending on T levels. Until recently, this prevailing wisdom regarding prostate cancer and testosterone had not been seriously questioned.

My Involvement in the Story

By the time I performed my urology training in the mid-1980s as a resident at the Harvard Program in Urology, based at the Brigham and Women's Hospital in Boston, one of the unassailable assumptions held by all the urologists I trained under was that prostate cancer shrunk with low T and grew with high T.

In my training, we learned that men who had been castrated early in life never developed prostate cancer. In the laboratory, prostate tumors could be placed under the skin on the back of mice, and the tumors would grow to a large size. Pieces of these tumors could then be transferred under the skin of another male animal and would again grow to a large size. If the males were castrated or given estrogen (which lowers testosterone), the tumor would shrink rapidly or not even take root.

The tumor would not grow at all, however, if it was transferred under the skin of a female. On the other hand, if the female were given testosterone, the tumor would grow just as well as if it had been placed in a male. All these studies indicated that testosterone was a critical element in allowing prostate cancer growth. There seemed to be good reason to believe that it would be dangerous to give testosterone supplementation to a man with prostate cancer. I believed that, and so did everyone around me.

My fellow residents and I thus learned to repeat the comments of our teachers to our patients in the clinics. Whenever issues of testosterone would come up, we would say the relationship of testosterone to prostate cancer was like "pouring gasoline on a fire" or providing "food for a hungry tumor." These phrases are still in use throughout the medical world.

In those days, we all spoke about testosterone and prostate cancer as if there were a simple, direct relationship, but the truth is not quite so simple.

A Fateful Interaction

Once I finished training, I began my specialization in the treatment of "guy stuff," primarily male infertility and sexual problems. I also began diagnosing and treating a large number of men with low T. This was not a common practice at the time; in fact, I had very little experience with T therapy during my training. This was because there was little research showing that testosterone treatment helped the symptoms seen in men with low T. Indeed, one of the most bothersome symptoms—erectile dysfunction—was believed at the time not to improve with testosterone treatment (later research has shown this belief to be incorrect). Doctors also were reluctant to prescribe testosterone because of the fear of promoting a prostate cancer that might be lurking silently inside the man's prostate gland.

At the end of my second year of practice, I ran into one of my former teachers at the national meeting of the American Urological Association. He asked me if it was true that I was treating men with testosterone. I replied that I was and explained that I had been pleasantly surprised to find so many good responders despite my earlier training.

"I wouldn't do that anymore, if I were you," he said. "I just had a patient diagnosed with prostate cancer within a year after beginning testosterone treatment. If you're going to continue treating men with testosterone, and I recommend you don't, you should at least do a prostate biopsy first to make sure they don't have cancer."

Naturally, this was a disconcerting conversation, especially coming from a former teacher of mine whom I respected greatly. So I followed his suggestion and began performing prostate biopsies before initiating T therapy. At least with a biopsy, I could rule out the presence of cancer.

At the time, the only reasons to do a prostate biopsy were for an abnormal-feeling prostate, as determined by a digital rectal exam (DRE), or for an abnormally high result for the prostate-specific antigen (PSA) blood test, which can indicate an increased risk of prostate cancer. Surprisingly, despite a normal DRE and PSA, one of the very first men I biopsied had cancer. This was very strange, because it was assumed at the time, as I've explained earlier, that a man with low T should have been protected against prostate cancer.

It didn't take long to find several more cancers in men with low T, despite normal DRE and PSA results. Indeed, of the first thirty-three men I biopsied, six had cancer. This was a very high cancer rate, especially for a group of men without known risk factors. After presenting these results at the national urology meeting, one of the academic chiefs, a well-respected man, declared in his trademark booming voice, "This is garbage! Everyone knows that high T causes prostate cancer, not low T. You guys just got unlucky. I bet if you biopsy the next 100 men, you won't find another cancer."

It was a dramatic moment—I was a young unknown being castigated on a national stage by a major figure in the field. And he was right—given what we knew about testosterone and prostate cancer, the results made no sense.

All I could do was respond, "These are the results we obtained. We present them here because they do fly in the face of conventional wisdom, which is why we believe they may be of interest to this audience."

When the size of the group we had biopsied was fifty men and the cancer rate was unchanged, my colleagues and I submitted a manuscript to the *Journal of the American Medical Association*, one of the top medical journals in the world. The associate editor soon called me up to say, "Our editorial board finds your data very interesting, because it runs counter to what we would expect.

But our concern is that your numbers are small, and perhaps you may have just had an unlucky run with your biopsies. If you gather additional men and your cancer rate holds up, we will seriously consider publishing your manuscript." Before long I submitted data on seventy-seven men, eleven of whom had cancer, and the paper was published.

At the time, in 1996, the 14 percent cancer rate we reported was several times greater than any previously reported cancer rate in men with normal PSA (4.0 ng/mL or less). Several studies had reported biopsy results in men with normal PSA with cancer rates of 0–4 percent, with the highest value reported being 4.5 percent. The much higher cancer rate in our population certainly seemed to suggest there was something different about prostate cancer risk in men with low T.

Frankly, most experts just didn't know what to make of our results. A high cancer rate among men with low T didn't fit into the existing way of thinking regarding testosterone and prostate cancer. And because we hadn't biopsied a control group of men (men with normal T and no other risk factors), it was impossible to say whether men with normal T would have had a different cancer rate than our patients with low T.

In retrospect, though, that paper was the first direct evidence in a major medical journal that standard assumptions about testosterone and prostate cancer might not be correct. At a minimum, it was obvious that low T could not be considered protective against the development of prostate cancer, as had been assumed for so long. And it made me wonder whether other assumptions about testosterone and prostate cancer were also incorrect.

The *New England Journal of Medicine*

After the publication of my article on prostate biopsies in men with low T, I published a number of additional articles looking at the relationship between testosterone and the prostate. In one provocative study, a colleague and I looked at whether T therapy posed special dangers for men who were already at high risk for developing prostate cancer.

In this study, we compared the results of T therapy given for twelve months in two groups of men with low T. The first group consisted of twenty men considered to be at high risk for prostate cancer based on biopsy results showing an allegedly precancerous condition called prostatic intraepithelial neoplasia (PIN). The second group consisted of fifty-five men with normal biopsy results. At the end of one year of treatment, both groups had a similar, modest increase in PSA. One man in the study, who was in the high-risk group, developed cancer.

So overall T therapy resulted in a one-year cancer rate of 1.3 percent (one of seventy-five men). More important, the one-year cancer rate among the high-risk men with PIN was 5 percent. This compared to the known cancer rate of 25 percent over three years in this population. While the two figures are not directly comparable, these results certainly did not seem to suggest that T therapy had increased the cancer rate in this high-risk group. And the overall cancer rate was not very high at all.

Here was another piece of evidence that the old assumptions about testosterone and prostate cancer were incorrect, specifically the notion that T therapy was like pouring gasoline on a fire. First, we had found that men with low T did not seem to be protected against developing cancer. Now, at the other extreme, we found that men at high risk for prostate cancer did not seem to suffer any dramatic "explosion" of cancer when treated for a year with T therapy. And when I looked back at my extensive experience of treating men with T therapy, many for ten years or longer, precious few cases of cancer had developed.

It was heresy, but I couldn't help thinking that the old stories linking testosterone levels to the risk of prostate cancer might well be wrong. After all, if one looks at the natural progression of prostate cancer, it never occurs in men in their twenties when T levels are at their lifetime peak, even though autopsy studies have shown that a significant percentage of these young men already harbor microscopic prostate cancers. Instead, prostate cancer becomes increasingly common as men age, when T levels have declined.

I was coming to the conclusion that the average physician might be unduly fearful of the risk of prostate cancer with T therapy. From my lectures to physicians around the country, it became clear to me that many physicians withheld T therapy from their patients because they feared stimulating a sleeping cancer. I thought it might be time to write a review article that put the risks of testosterone in perspective, particularly the risk of prostate cancer. Fortunately for me, the *New England Journal of Medicine* was receptive to my proposal to consider such a publication.

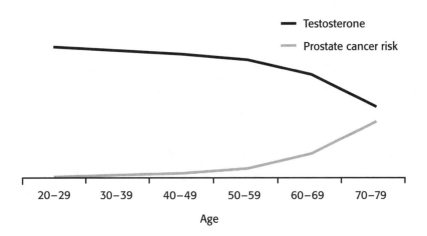

── Testosterone

▬▬ Prostate cancer risk

Age

20–29   30–39   40–49   50–59   60–69   70–79

Prostate Cancer Prevalence Increases as Testosterone Levels Decline

Although it has been widely believed for several decades that higher testosterone levels are associated with prostate cancer risk, it turns out there is no scientific evidence that this is true. On the contrary, as this figure shows, men are at increased risk for prostate cancer when they are older and their T levels have declined. Men never develop prostate cancer when they are young and their T levels are at their lifetime peak. New evidence suggests that low T, rather than high T, may be a risk for prostate cancer.

The *New England Journal of Medicine* is arguably the most prestigious medical journal in the world, and its reputation stems in part from publishing only the best-researched articles. Together with Dr. Ernani Rhoden, a urology professor from Brazil who came to Boston to do a yearlong research fellowship with me, I spent a year reviewing all the available scientific and medical literature on the risks of testosterone treatment to be able to provide a manuscript that lived up to such standards. Once we had written up the manuscript, our paper was subjected to multiple waves of reviews by physicians from various specialties—urology, oncology, endocrinology—to make sure that we had not left out any key studies or misrepresented any of the data.

The first thing we looked at was the rate of prostate cancer in men undergoing treatment with testosterone. Although many of the studies were small, the cumulative cancer rate in these trials was only slightly higher than 1 percent. This cancer rate was actually less than the cancer detection rate in men undergoing screening for prostate cancer. However, there was no large, long-term study looking at cancer rates in men receiving T therapy and comparing them to men who did not receive T therapy; thus, by themselves, these studies could not provide a definitive conclusion regarding risk.

There also were some large, sophisticated studies that indirectly addressed the risk of testosterone and prostate cancer. Unlike the studies I just mentioned, in which men given T treatment were monitored for the development of prostate cancer, these large studies simply looked to see if there was a connection between a man's own natural level of testosterone and his risk of developing prostate cancer. In these observational studies, blood samples were taken and frozen at the beginning of the study, and then the large study group was followed for long periods of time. At the end of the study period, often ten to twenty years later, a group of men would have developed prostate cancer. The blood samples obtained from these men at the beginning of the study would then be tested for testosterone and other hormones and compared to a similar group of men who were matched for age and other characteristics but who did not develop prostate cancer. What did they find?

In 2004, when my article in the *New England Journal of Medicine* was published, there were fifteen of these longitudinal studies examining the relationship of hormones and prostate cancer. Since 2004, there have been approximately a half-dozen more. Not one has shown any direct relationship between the level of total testosterone in a man's blood and the subsequent likelihood that he will develop prostate cancer. Specifically, average total T levels were not higher in the cancer group compared to men without cancer, and men with the highest T values were at no greater risk for later developing prostate cancer than men with the lowest T values.

Among the dozens of additional calculations in each of these studies, an occasional minor correlation did show up, such as a connection with the minor androgen DHEA in one, a ratio of testosterone to SHBG in another, or a calculated free T in a third. But in all cases so far, attempts to confirm these minor connections have failed.

At the end of immersing ourselves into this literature for a full year, Rhoden and I were stunned by the fact that there was not a single study in human patients to suggest that raising testosterone increased the risk of prostate cancer. Although I was fairly convinced at this point that T therapy was not a risk for prostate cancer, I had to admit that the evidence was not absolutely conclusive. And there was still a widespread belief that T therapy was risky. And so our relatively sanitized conclusion appeared as follows:

Thus, there appears to be no compelling evidence at present to suggest that men with higher testosterone levels are at greater risk of prostate cancer or that treating men who have hypogonadism with exogenous androgens increases this risk.

Our article appeared in the *New England Journal of Medicine* in 2004. Whatever the truth may turn out to be regarding testosterone and prostate cancer, it was clear that raising testosterone did not appear to be like "food for a hungry tumor." Physicians who had been interested in offering T therapy to their patients but were worried about the cancer risk now had a reference article that gave them some degree of comfort.

Later that same year, the Institute of Medicine, a branch of the National Academy of Sciences, published its recommendations regarding testosterone research in aging men, with an eye toward ensuring the safety of men participating in testosterone studies. Recognizing the disparity between the concern that testosterone stimulates prostate cancer and the lack of any strong supporting evidence, the report concluded: "In summary, the influence of testosterone on prostate carcinogenesis and other prostate outcomes remains poorly defined . . ." The unwillingness of the report's authors to identify testosterone as a definite risk for prostate cancer was a major departure from the standard story line that had colored earlier discussions of T therapy, and it served as a nice bookend to our article on testosterone risks in the *New England Journal of Medicine*.

Discoveries in the Basement of the Countway Medical Library

As much as my yearlong review of the scientific literature had given me confidence that testosterone therapy did not increase the risk of developing prostate cancer, there were still a few issues that disturbed me.

The first was the original observation by Huggins himself that administration of testosterone to men caused "enhanced growth" of prostate cancer in men with metastatic disease. A second was a well-known 1981 article from the Memorial Sloan-Kettering Cancer Center in New York, authored by the most prominent prostate cancer expert of his era, Dr. Willet Whitmore, that reported near-universal poor outcomes when men with metastatic prostate cancer received testosterone injections. And the third was the phenomenon known as testosterone flare. Testosterone flare refers to the temporary increase in testosterone caused by the use of medications called LHRH agonists in men with advanced prostate cancer. Testosterone flare has been associated with a variety of complications attributed to the sudden growth of prostate cancer.

All three of these issues applied only to men with known metastatic disease, and because no one was suggesting that T therapy be offered to men with advanced prostate cancer, the existence of this literature wasn't terribly troubling. What was of concern to those of us prescribing testosterone therapy was the possibility that we might be putting our otherwise healthy patients at risk for prostate cancer, but so far all the data looked reassuring on this point. Metastatic disease was something quite different, and it would not have been shocking to learn that it responded differently to high levels of testosterone than localized disease within the prostate.

But I was still bothered.

I had read all the relevant articles years ago during my training, but not with a critical eye toward the relationship of testosterone and prostate cancer. One day, I found myself with an unexpectedly free afternoon and decided to investigate. Everything changed for me the day I descended into the basement of the Countway Library, Harvard Medical School's incredible archive of medical literature. It was the most exciting day of my professional career, a day that changed my views on testosterone, prostate cancer, and, even more, on medicine itself.

The Original Huggins Article

The basement of Countway Library is where the old volumes of medical journals are kept. Some of these, from august journals such as *The Lancet*, go back to the 1800s. It is an amazing collection, open to any member of the Harvard community.

I found the original article by Huggins from 1941. It was in the very first published volume of what is now a highly respected journal called *Cancer Research*. I read how Dr. Huggins and his coinvestigator, Clarence Hodges, used the new blood test called acid phosphatase to show that lowering testosterone by castration or estrogen treatment caused prostate cancer to regress, and how T injections had caused "enhanced growth" of prostate cancer in these men. And then I noticed something that made my heart race.

Huggins and Hodges had written that three men had received T injections. But results were given for only two men. And one of these men had already been castrated. This meant that there were results for only a single man who had received T injections without prior hormonal manipulation. Dr. Huggins had based his "enhanced growth" conclusion on a single patient, using a test—acid phosphatase—that has since been abandoned because it provided such erratic results!

I sat there in the basement of the library, reading the same lines over and over to make sure I hadn't misread it. Later, I asked several colleagues to read it as well. Dr. Huggins's assertion that higher testosterone caused greater growth of prostate cancer, repeated for so long and accepted as gospel, was based on almost nothing at all!

The Memorial Sloan-Kettering Experience

I was still giddy when I decided to look up the article detailing the experience of testosterone administration to men with metastatic disease from the Memorial Sloan-Kettering Cancer Center, published in 1981 by the urologic giant of his day, Willet Whitmore, and his colleague, Jackson Fowler. The short summary of the paper was quite damning. Over a course of eighteen years, fifty-two men with metastatic disease had undergone treatment with daily T injections, usually as a last-gasp treatment for their cancer. Of these fifty-two men, forty-five had experienced an "unfavorable response," most within the first month of treatment.

This seemed pretty grim. Maybe Huggins had been right after all, despite basing his conclusions on a solitary patient. But then I discovered something equally shocking in the fine print of this article. Of the fifty-two men studied, all but four had already been treated with castration or estrogen treatment to lower testosterone. And of these four previously untreated men, one had an early, unspecified unfavorable response, while the remaining three men continued to receive daily T injections for 52, 55, and 310 days without apparent negative effects. In fact, one of these men was reported to have had a "favorable response" to T administration.

Drs. Fowler and Whitmore were impressed by the difference in outcomes for the untreated group of four men compared with the men who had already undergone hormonal treatment to lower testosterone. To explain the lack of negative effects on the untreated men, the authors postulated the following: "Normal endogenous testosterone levels may be sufficient to cause near maximal stimulation of prostatic tumors." In other words, raising T levels beyond the normal range did not seem to cause any increased cancer growth, even in men with metastatic disease!

This important concept was lost in the headline of the study, which clearly indicated that giving testosterone to men with prostate cancer was associated with rapid onset of negative consequences in most men. One had to read the article closely to learn that the headline applied only to men who had been previously castrated. Although this article has been cited for many years as evidence that T administration causes rapid and near-universal growth of prostate cancer (PCa), the authors in fact clearly made the point that the worrisome effects of T administration did *not* appear to occur in their small group of men without prior hormonal treatment.

Testosterone Flare

It had been an amazing day in the library, which had long since turned to night. My head was spinning, but I wanted to tackle the last hurdle, the problem of testosterone flare. In the early 1980s, medications were developed to replace the need for surgical removal of the testicles for men with advanced prostate cancer. These medications are called LHRH agonists, and they continue to be used to this day. LHRH injections cause T concentrations to increase by 50 percent or more for seven to ten days, after which testosterone levels fall rapidly to castrate levels. This transient rise in testosterone is called testosterone flare.

Not long after LHRH agonists began to be used, there were reports of complications occurring after men began these treatments, and these complications were attributed to testosterone flare causing rapid growth of prostate cancer. These complications included the inability to urinate, worsening of bone pain, or, in the most tragic cases, paralysis due to collapse of a vertebra in which the cancer had eaten away the bone. As a result, for the last twenty years, it has been routine to add medications to block testosterone flare when starting a patient on treatment with LHRH agonists.

That night in the basement of Countway Library, I pulled all the original studies I could find on LHRH agonists, as well as reports of bad outcomes due to the flare. As I read, two things became apparent. First, many of the bad outcomes attributed to testosterone flare occurred a month or more after initiation of treatment. This meant that these complications occurred not when T levels were high, but when T levels had already dropped for some time to castrate levels.

Second, out of the substantial literature on LHRH agonists and prostate cancer, I could find only two articles that actually measured and reported PSA levels during the time of the testosterone flare. And here was the kicker: both articles showed absolutely no change in mean PSA values during the time of the testosterone flare! Curiously, neither article so much as mentioned this result.

PSA is an excellent indicator of prostate cancer growth. The fact that PSA did not rise in these men during the testosterone flare strongly suggested that the cancers did not grow during this time. Perhaps the complications attributed to testosterone flare were nothing more than the cancer progression that would have happened without any treatment at all.

It had been quite a day and night in the Countway Library. I left with my head spinning and a feeling that I had stumbled onto something very important. It was like the children's story "The Emperor's New Clothes"—we see what we want to see. And for two-thirds of a century, it had been assumed that raising testosterone increased prostate cancer growth. But maybe the emperor was naked.

Even in men with metastatic disease, there was no evidence I could find that raising testosterone made prostate cancer grow more than it would have anyway. Shockingly, the very publications cited so regularly to demonstrate a dangerous relationship between testosterone and prostate cancer contained evidence that this was not true.

The Paradox Resolved

Still, I was worried, because there was a bothersome unresolved paradox to explain. For decades, the story line was that lowering testosterone levels caused prostate cancer to shrink away and raising testosterone levels caused it to grow. The second part of this story was now seriously in doubt, yet the first part was obviously correct. In my own practice, I had seen the beneficial effects of lowering testosterone levels many times over in men with advanced prostate cancer. This part of Dr. Huggins's work was indisputable. But if lowering testosterone levels caused these cancers to shrink, how was it possible that raising testosterone levels did not cause the cancers to grow? This was a paradox that needed to be solved if physicians were to accept the possibility that T therapy may not increase the risk of prostate cancer.

The answer turns out to be not all that complicated. All the reports of testosterone causing rapid growth of prostate cancer occurred in men who already had extremely low testosterone levels, due to castration or estrogen treatment. Once we get beyond the near-castrate range, it is hard to find any evidence that changes in T concentrations matter at all to prostate cancer. This is essentially what Drs. Fowler and Whitmore described in their 1981 article when they suggested that "near maximal" growth of prostate cancer is provided by naturally occurring T concentrations.

The experimental proof of this concept was provided by a landmark article published in 2006 using much more sophisticated means. In this study by Leonard Marks and colleagues, men with low T received injections of testosterone or a placebo every two weeks for a total of six months. At the beginning and end of the study, measurements of testosterone and DHT (the more active form of testosterone within prostate tissue) were obtained from the blood and also from the prostate itself. The results showed that although blood concentrations of testosterone and DHT rose substantially in the T injection group, as expected, the concentration of testosterone and DHT within the prostate itself did not change at all and was similar to the group that received placebo injections. In addition, biochemical markers of prostate cell growth also did not change with T injections.

This study showed in elegant fashion that raising T levels in the blood did not raise T levels within the prostate. It is as if once the prostate has been exposed to enough testosterone, any additional testosterone is treated as excess and does not accumulate in the prostate. In technical terms, we say the prostate has been saturated with regard to testosterone. And it is this saturation that resolves the paradox of testosterone and prostate cancer.

Saturation explains the paradox in this way. At very low levels of T, near the castrate range, prostate growth is very sensitive to changes in T concentration. Thus, severely lowering testosterone will definitely cause prostate cancer to shrink; adding testosterone back will cause the cancer to regrow. However, once we get above the point where the prostate is saturated with testosterone, adding more testosterone will have little, if any, further impact on prostate cancer growth. Experimental studies suggest the concentration at which this saturation occurs is quite low.

In other words, the old analogy I learned in training was false. Testosterone is not like food for a hungry tumor. Instead, a much better analogy is, "Testosterone is like water for a thirsty tumor." Once the thirst has been satisfied, prostate tumors have no use for additional testosterone. And the vast majority of men with low T appear to have prostates that are not particularly thirsty.

A New Concern: Prostate Cancer and Low Testosterone

I no longer fear that giving a man T therapy will make a hidden prostate cancer grow or put him at increased risk of developing prostate cancer down the road. My real concern now is that men with *low* T are at an *increased* risk of already having prostate cancer.

When my colleagues and I published our results in 1996 from prostate biopsies in men with low T and PSA of 4.0 ng/mL or less, the 14 percent cancer rate was several times higher than any published series of men with normal PSA. In 2006, Dr. Rhoden and I published a larger study of prostate biopsies performed in

345 men. The cancer rate of 15 percent in this group was very similar to the first study. But whereas the cancer rate in 1996 was much higher than anything published to that date in men with PSA of 4.0 ng/mL or less, in 2006 the perspective had changed due to an important study called the Prostate Cancer Prevention Trial.

In that study, the cancer rate among men with a PSA of 4.0 ng/mL or less was also 15 percent. Because this value is identical to what we had found in our patients with low T, it was suggested that the cancer rate in men with low T is the same as the normal population—neither higher nor lower. However, the average age of men in our study was a decade younger than the men studied in the Prostate Cancer Prevention Trial (fifty-nine versus sixty-nine years). Almost half the men in the other study were seventy years or older, and age is the greatest risk factor we know for prostate cancer. The way I look at these numbers is that men with low T have a cancer rate as high as men with normal T who are a decade older.

More important, in our study of 345 men, we found that the degree of testosterone deficiency correlated with the degree of cancer risk. Men whose T levels were in the bottom third of the group were twice as likely to have cancer diagnosed on biopsy as men in the upper third. This finding adds to the concern that low T is a risk factor for prostate cancer.

There is now additional data from around the world associating low T and worrisome features of prostate cancer. For example, low T is associated with more aggressive tumors. In addition, men with low T appear to have a more advanced stage of disease at the time of surgical treatment.

Whereas I originally began to perform prostate biopsies in men with low T because I was worried that treatment might cause a hidden cancer to grow, I now perform biopsies in these men because I am concerned they might have an increased risk of cancer. This risk is approximately one in seven for men with PSA values less than 4.0 ng/mL.

Because prostate cancer tends to be curable when caught early, I feel I've done these men a service by finding their cancers before they have an abnormal PSA or DRE. With today's ability to monitor men with prostate cancer, not all of these men will necessarily require treatment. But the ones who have evidence of more aggressive tumors should definitely have an advantage by having their diagnosis made early.

The Evidence as It Now Stands

For over sixty-five years, there has been a fear that T therapy will cause new prostate cancers to arise or hidden ones to grow. Although no large-scale studies have yet been performed to provide a definitive verdict on the safety of T therapy, it is quite remarkable to discover that the long-standing fear about testosterone and prostate cancer has little scientific support. The old concepts, taken as gospel, do not stand up to critical examination. I believe the best summary about the risk of prostate cancer from T therapy, based on published evidence at the time this book is written, is as follows:

- Low blood levels of testosterone do not protect against prostate cancer and, indeed, may increase the risk.
- High blood levels of testosterone do not increase the risk of prostate cancer.
- Treatment with testosterone does not increase the risk of prostate cancer, even among men who are already at high risk for it.
- In men who do have metastatic prostate cancer and who have been given treatment that drops their blood levels of testos-

terone to near zero, starting treatment with testosterone (or stopping treatment that has lowered their testosterone to near zero) *might* increase the risk that residual cancer will again start to grow.

One of the most important and reassuring studies regarding testosterone and prostate cancer was an article published in the *Journal of the National Cancer Institute* in 2008, in which the authors of eighteen separate studies from around the world pooled their data regarding the likelihood of developing prostate cancer based on concentrations of various hormones, including testosterone. This enormous study included more than 3,000 men with prostate cancer and more than 6,000 men without prostate cancer, who served as controls in the study. No relationship was found between prostate cancer and any of the hormones studied, including total testosterone, free testosterone, or other minor androgens. In an accompanying editorial, Dr. William Carpenter and colleagues from the University of North Carolina School of Public Health suggest that scientists finally move beyond the long-believed but unsupported view that high T is a risk for prostate cancer.

More and more physicians are coming around to recognize that T therapy is not a true risk for prostate cancer, but it can take many years to alter established beliefs. Don't be surprised if your own doctor still raises this issue with you if you are considering T therapy. If he objects to treating you for that reason, you should refer him to the article just mentioned, or one of the other review articles listed in References at the back of this book. Even better, have him read this chapter!

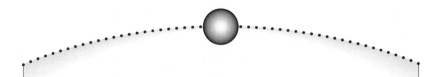

Questions and Answers

Q. *I'm fifty-three years old and I've been on testosterone therapy for two years, with good results. However, my father was diagnosed with prostate cancer at age seventy-five. Does this mean I need to stop testosterone?*

A. There is a familial form of prostate cancer, but only in families in which prostate cancer occurs at age sixty-five or younger. Even in those families where a family member develops cancer at a young age, this does not necessarily mean that every other male in the family will develop cancer. Men with a family history of prostate cancer should be sure to have a yearly PSA and prostate exam. There is no need to discontinue testosterone treatment.

Q. *My physician started me on testosterone, but I never had a prostate biopsy. I am sixty-four years old. Was this a mistake?*

A. Because there is no evidence that testosterone treatment increases the risk of prostate cancer, it is fine to begin therapy as long as your PSA and DRE are normal. My own practice is to recommend prostate biopsy in men with low T because our published data indicate there is an increased risk that cancer is already present in men with low T, but this is by no means a standard recommendation yet among physicians.

Q. *Why do you perform prostate biopsies on men with low T if you don't feel that testosterone treatment will make a hidden cancer grow?*

A. Because so many men with prostate cancer will not die from it, even without treatment, there is a fair amount of controversy over how aggressive to be in making the diagnosis. My perspective is that it is worth knowing the diagnosis, whether or not one chooses to be treated immediately. And because low T seems to represent a small but definite increased risk, I feel that biopsy in men over fifty with low T is worthwhile.

Q. *A man in my bowling league was started on testosterone treatment and then developed prostate cancer one year later. Doesn't that show that testosterone is risky for prostate cancer?*

A. If the wife of this man had switched to a new type of laundry detergent before the cancer was diagnosed, would we assume the cancer was caused by the detergent? Of course not. But we are predisposed to believe that T therapy causes prostate cancer, so it is easy to hear a story like this and assume that T therapy caused the cancer. Prostate cancer and T therapy are both common in the United States, and both tend to occur in the same age range, so there will always be stories of men developing cancer some time after beginning T therapy. If testosterone really made prostate cancers grow, then we should see high rates of cancer among men who start testosterone therapy. But we don't. It's false logic.

Q. *Isn't it true that all men would eventually get prostate cancer if they lived long enough? If so, why does it even matter if testosterone were to increase the risk of something that is inevitable anyway?*

A. Men do get prostate cancer at an increasingly high rate as they age. And it is true that most men diagnosed with prostate cancer would never have a moment's trouble from it, even if it were left untreated, because most of these cancers grow so slowly that other medical conditions eventually become more troublesome. Yet for those with more aggressive forms of prostate cancer, the danger is very real. The challenge is to identify men at risk, because even high-grade prostate cancer is curable when caught early.

Q. *It took more than thirty years for scientists to learn that hormones were dangerous for women and caused breast cancer. Isn't it possible we'll eventually find out the same is true for testosterone and prostate cancer?*

A. The fear that hormone therapy is dangerous in women is currently being reevaluated, and it appears to not be as dangerous as was originally proclaimed. More to the point, it is critical to understand that men are not women and that testosterone is not estrogen. Anyone, particularly a scientist, must always allow for the possibility that new information will one day change current views. But after so much research over so many decades, there is little reason to believe that T therapy poses a major risk for prostate cancer. As a medical student once said to me, "If testosterone is really so dangerous for prostate cancer, why is it so hard to show it?"

Chapter 8

Risks, Side Effects, and Medical Monitoring

Every medical treatment known to man has some risk or potential for side effects, and testosterone treatment is no different. However, testosterone differs from nearly all other medical treatments in that treatment involves simply adding back to the body a chemical that is already present, albeit in reduced amounts. For this reason, testosterone treatment is often referred to as testosterone supplementation.

Unlike estrogen pills used to treat women, almost all of which differ from the natural chemical but have similar effects, testosterone preparations are made of exactly the same molecule as the testosterone found normally in the body. The exception is the oral forms of testosterone, which are only rarely used because of their potential to cause liver damage. Because T therapy consists in raising the blood concentration of the same molecule found in the body naturally, the side effects or risks of T therapy should in theory be nothing more than having increased concentrations of testosterone. This is true to a great extent and explains the very reassuring safety record for T treatment, but there are still instances where different reactions may occur. Before beginning T treatment, it is important to be aware of what those risks might be.

I've already discussed the concern about prostate cancer in the last chapter, so I won't go over it again here, other than to repeat that the evidence fails to support the long-held concerns that higher testosterone might increase the risk of prostate cancer or that it might cause a hidden, undetected prostate cancer to grow. A considerable amount of information now indicates that testosterone is quite safe for the prostate.

Over the years, there have been a number of concerns raised about T therapy that have proven to be without substance (e.g., heart disease or prostate cancer) or that relate to the use of older types of T formulations (e.g., liver toxicity with oral testosterone). I include them here together with the proven risks and side effects so that you can understand the issues in case you come across these concerns from your physician or from other sources of information.

Heart Disease

Men have more heart attacks and heart disease than women at any given age, and there has been a concern that higher testosterone may be the culprit because men have more testosterone than women do. Fortunately, this concern appears to be unfounded. In fact, recent evidence suggests that it is actually men with *low* T who are at increased risk of heart disease.

One of the original stories that propelled the concern about testosterone and heart disease was the published case about thirty years ago of a forty-year-old bodybuilder who died suddenly, apparently from a heart attack. He had been taking high doses of steroids, and because heart attacks are rare at such a young age, it was assumed that his steroid use must have been the cause. Today, we recognize that sudden cardiac deaths can happen in young men who have never been suspected of taking testosterone, so the connection seems less worrisome. In addition, multiple studies using very high doses of testosterone that raised concentrations well above the normal range have not caused any heart attacks or other heart problems, and this has greatly quieted the concern about testosterone and heart disease.

Another reason there had been concern about testosterone and heart disease was that a small number of medical articles appeared to link high T concentrations with increased total cholesterol or LDL cholesterol, the "bad" cholesterol. However, multiple studies have now shown that T therapy either affects cholesterol very little or in a positive way. A closer look at the original reports revealed that it was only high-dose injections leading to above-normal blood levels or oral forms of testosterone that were associated with increased cholesterol levels. Today, the cholesterol "story" with T therapy has been put to rest. Whereas it was once recommended that men receiving T therapy should have their cholesterol levels checked on a regular basis, this recommendation has now been abandoned by nearly all published guidelines and recommendations.

Atherosclerosis is another way to look at heart disease risk. Atherosclerosis is the medical term for what is known as "hardening of the arteries" and refers to the clogging of blood vessels with plaque that makes it more difficult for blood to flow freely within blood vessels. It is the number one cause of heart attacks and strokes, as well as arterial disease throughout the body.

In one study conducted in Rotterdam, 504 men were screened for the presence of severe atherosclerosis in the aorta, using ultrasound. When these men were grouped into three equal groups on the basis of their T levels, it turned out that the group with the highest testosterone levels had the lowest risk of atherosclerosis, while the group with the lowest testosterone levels had the highest risk. In fact, the risk of severe atherosclerosis among men with the highest T levels was only one-fifth as great as men with the lowest T levels. In other words, low T was a risk for atherosclerosis, and higher concentrations of testosterone appeared to be protective.

In addition, there is growing evidence that normal levels of testosterone may actually be helpful for the heart. In one study, men with low T and angina (chest pain due to heart disease) were studied after being treated with either T gel or placebo. At the end of the treatment period, men on T therapy were able to exercise significantly longer without development of angina compared with men who received placebo.

As with the prostate cancer story, we lack a large-scale, long-term study on T therapy, so it is impossible to make a definitive statement about the risk of T therapy with regard to heart disease. On the other hand, there is now a moderately large set of evidence that not only rejects the idea that T therapy is bad for the heart, but that strongly suggests that normal levels of testosterone may be beneficial for the heart.

Erythrocytosis (Overabundance of Red Blood Cells)

Testosterone helps to stimulate red blood cell production. Thus, for several decades, testosterone treatment was used to help men with anemia (too few red blood cells) due to bone marrow disease or kidney failure. On average, the hematocrit (the percentage of blood composed of red blood cells) rises 3 percent with T therapy.

What may be helpful for a man with anemia (a low hematocrit) may be troublesome for another man whose hematocrit was normal to begin with, especially if his hematocrit was near the upper limit of normal when he started T therapy. In these men, the hematocrit can rise too high, a condition called erythrocytosis.

The danger of erythrocytosis is that the blood can become too viscous, or thick, predisposing a person to clogged arteries, which in turn could lead to a stroke or a heart attack.

Erythrocytosis is a real risk of T therapy, and for this reason men receiving T therapy should have their hematocrit or hemoglobin checked at least twice during the first year, and at least once yearly thereafter. Fortunately, erythrocytosis resolves fairly quickly once T therapy is stopped or if the dose is reduced.

Erythrocytosis occurs almost exclusively in men using injections and is quite rare in men using T patches and gels. It is believed that the transient high concentrations achieved with injections are responsible for the greater risk of erythrocytosis.

Practically speaking, if the hematocrit rises above 54 percent, or if the hemoglobin (an alternative test favored by some physicians) rises above 18, then it is time to temporarily stop treatment or lower the dose. A few of my patients donate blood on a regular basis as a way to keep their hematocrit in a reasonable range, while simultaneously doing a good deed.

Infertility

It bears repeating that T therapy can lower sperm counts for men, often to zero, resulting in temporary infertility. For this reason, any man considering T therapy should be asked whether he is interested in fathering a child sometime in the near future. If he is, then T gels, patches, and injections should not be prescribed. Instead, oral medications that raise a man's natural production of testosterone, such as clomiphene citrate or anastrozole, should be prescribed. If symptoms don't respond as well as desired, the more standard forms of T therapy can be prescribed once the wife or partner is pregnant.

Although good T levels are necessary to produce reasonable numbers of sperm, raising testosterone with gels, patches, and injections stimulate the negative feedback system to reduce LH secretion, which in turn shuts down the testicular production of testosterone. Low T within the testicles causes the sperm machinery to go to sleep. By no means does this mean that men on T therapy can stop using contraceptive measures—many men will still have sperm, albeit very low numbers, and the presence of any sperm runs the risk of an unwanted pregnancy.

I can't begin to tell you how many men I've seen in the office for an infertility evaluation, who have low or absent sperm counts and who include some form of T therapy on their medication list. It is not uncommon for physicians to neglect to mention the suppressive effect of T therapy on fertility. It's easy to forget that some older men have younger wives and that they may wish to have children together. Fortunately, nearly all the men I've seen with zero or low sperm counts while on T therapy will have good sperm values again three to six months after stopping T therapy.

Reduction in Testicular Size

Rarely, men on T therapy may notice that their testicles are smaller or less firm than before treatment. This softening or shrinkage of the testicles occurs because of the reduction in sperm production within the testicles, as described previously. The change in testicular size is usually mild and not noticeable. Occasionally, I have had a patient who is bothered by it, in which case switching to clomiphene citrate or anastrozole should be considered. The effect on the testicles is reversible once treatment is stopped.

Fluid Retention

A very small number of men on testosterone treatment may retain fluid. This means that caution must be exercised for men with heart failure, kidney failure, or advanced liver disease. An occasional patient has told me that his weight increases for the first few days after receiving a T injection, then declines back to normal. I have never had a patient of mine develop swelling of the feet or legs from T therapy, but this rare complication has been reported by others.

Liver Damage

The standard forms of T therapy (injections, gels, and patches) do not cause any liver problems. However, all testosterone products contain a warning that T therapy can cause liver damage. This is because the oral forms of testosterone do pose this risk, and the FDA requires all testosterone products to share the same language regarding risks. The primary reason the oral forms of testosterone are not prescribed for low T is precisely because they can be dangerous for the liver.

Published guidelines and recommendations no longer suggest monitoring liver function while receiving T therapy, because of the reassuring data regarding liver function with the standard forms of T therapy.

Acne

Testosterone treatment can increase the oil production of glands in the skin, leading to acne. This is usually mild and will generally subside after the first several months of treatment.

High Blood Pressure

High blood pressure, technically called hypertension, is one of the most common medical conditions in men. Numerous studies have shown that T therapy does not influence blood pressure in men, and the guidelines of the Endocrine Society do not make any recommendation that blood pressure should be monitored after beginning T therapy. However, there are scattered, rare reports of blood pressure rising with T therapy and then returning to normal when treatment was stopped. Perhaps these rare individuals are sensitive to the fluid-retaining properties of testosterone that affect some men.

Rash

Skin irritation can occur with any kind of cream or other topical treatment. Although testosterone itself does not appear to be a problem for the skin, the agents used to help testosterone be absorbed through the skin via patches and gels can certainly cause a rash. In fact, one of the limiting features of the T patches is that they cause red blotches at the application site in a third or more of men who use them. Skin rashes can also occur with gels, but this happens infrequently, in no more than 1 percent of cases.

The rash seen with patches consists of a red, itchy area where the product has been applied to the skin, which usually fades over two to three days without treatment. Pretreating the area with steroid cream before application of the patch can reduce skin irritation. Men who develop bothersome rashes with T patches or gels usually do better with a different mode of T therapy.

Benign Growth of the Prostate and Urinary Problems

Just as physicians have worried for decades that higher testosterone levels would cause growth of prostate cancer (see Chapter 7), so too has it been assumed that T therapy would cause benign growth of the prostate. This enlargement of the prostate, often referred to as benign prostatic hyperplasia (BPH) occurs normally in men with age. It is responsible for the near-universal experience of older men that their urinary stream is slower and less powerful, and it can also cause frequent and urgent urination.

The worry about worsening BPH with T therapy comes from the fact that castration will also shrink the benign prostate, as it does the cancerous prostate. And in similar fashion to the evidence regarding prostate cancer (see Chapter 7), multiple studies have failed to show that the size of the benign prostate enlarges substantially with T therapy. Even more important, multiple studies have shown that urinary flow rates and other measures of urinary function do not change and that symptoms also do not change.

Although some experts have warned against the use of T therapy in men with severe symptoms of BPH, there is no scientific literature to support this recommendation.

Breast Enlargement

Breast enlargement in men, called gynecomastia, can be a sign of low T, as well as a rare side effect of treatment with testosterone. When it occurs as a sign of low T, the enlargement is usually due to fatty tissue and can improve or even disappear in some cases with T therapy, due to loss of fatty tissue.

Rarely, T therapy itself can cause gynecomastia by stimulating growth of gland tissue in the breast itself. This occurs because of conversion of testosterone into estrogen, which in turn stimulates the growth of breast tissue. Tenderness of the nipple or breast area or actual growth of breast tissue can obviously be very distressing to a man. Thankfully, this side effect of T therapy is extremely uncommon, and the tenderness and swelling disappear once T therapy is stopped.

If a man wishes to continue with T therapy, the breast swelling can be successfully treated by use of a medication, anastrozole, that blocks conversion of testosterone to estrogen. Other treatments include surgical removal of the breast tissue or a single low-dose radiation treatment.

Altered Mood

One of the pervasive myths about T therapy is that it can induce unpredictable or even violent behavior in men. This story comes from the world of bodybuilders, from reports in that population of what has been called "'roid rage" after taking extremely high doses of steroids. However—and this is important—this 'roid rage does not appear to apply to men using normal doses of T therapy for symptoms of low T. Even at doses of testosterone that far exceed the normal range, medical studies have not reported this type of violent, unpredictable behavior or bizarre mood.

It's a point not always appreciated, but the world of illicit steroid use for body or performance enhancement cannot be directly compared to the treatment of men with low T. The usual regimen of steroid users includes multiple drugs, at doses that can be twenty times the upper limit of T concentrations found in nature. Frequently, the steroids used were intended for veterinary, not human, use. We know little about the physical and psychological effects of these drug regimens because they have not been studied medically or scientifically. Yet many people assume that experiences of bodybuilders and other steroid-using athletes apply to men on T therapy. This is an incorrect assumption.

In fact, T therapy appears to act as a mood stabilizer or a mood enhancer in most studies. In animals such as stags, unpredictable, aggressive behavior is noted during periods of the year when testosterone is lowest. In humans, low T is associated with crankiness or irritability, and these symptoms are often alleviated by T therapy.

Nevertheless, I have had the occasional patient who has reported experiencing "a shorter fuse" after beginning T therapy. It can be difficult to tell in these cases whether T therapy restored an earlier personality feature or whether the shorter fuse was truly a side effect of T therapy itself. Mood disorders are not considered a side effect of T therapy and are not listed as such by the guidelines of the Endocrine Society.

Factors to Monitor While on Testosterone Therapy

If you are receiving T therapy, there are several things your physician should be checking regularly while you are on treatment. The items that need to be followed are:

- The prostate
- Testosterone levels
- Hematocrit and hemoglobin
- Bone density

The Prostate

Although there is solid evidence that T therapy will not cause any trouble for the prostate, this remains a controversial point. And because men at risk for development of BPH or prostate cancer overlap with men at risk for having low T, it makes sense to monitor the prostate before and during T therapy. My own practice is to perform a prostate biopsy prior to beginning T therapy because the evidence suggests there is a small but definite increased risk of cancer among men with low T (see Chapter 7). An alternative, preferred by most physicians, is to monitor the prostate at regular intervals with the prostate-specific antigen (PSA) blood test and an examination of the prostate.

Men with low T should have a prostate exam (often called a digital rectal exam) and the PSA blood test before beginning treatment, once or twice during the first year of treatment, and then at least once yearly thereafter. A prostate biopsy should be performed for any worrisome findings or for a substantial increase in PSA during the course of treatment.

Interpreting PSA and the Prostate Exam. Any significant changes in the digital rectal exam (DRE) or a substantial rise in PSA requires evaluation by a urologist and possibly a prostate biopsy to make sure the change is not due to cancer. During the DRE, the physician is looking for lumps or for an area that feels different from the rest of the prostate. General, smooth enlargement of the prostate is not worrisome, as this is something that happens with age in most men and is not a sign of cancer.

The PSA story is more complicated. PSA is a chemical made by normal prostate tissue, but it is also made by prostate cancer. In general, the higher the PSA, the greater the concern that cancer is present. PSA levels tend to rise with age, corresponding to greater amounts of prostate tissue due to benign enlargement. A slow, gradual rise in PSA over several years is not alarming, but an unusually rapid rise in PSA can be a worrisome indicator of cancer.

Until the last several years, PSA levels of less than 4.0 ng/mL were considered fine, but now many experts consider 2.5 ng/mL as the upper limit of normal. This means that a prostate biopsy should be considered for a man with a PSA of 2.6 ng/mL or higher, regardless of whether he has low T or has been using T therapy. Most physicians will relax this recommendation for men older than seventy-five, recommending a biopsy in these men only for much higher levels of PSA.

As a recommendation for men about to start T therapy, the most prudent practice is to perform a biopsy if the starting PSA is greater than 2.5 ng/mL or if the PSA rises above 2.5 ng/mL during the course of treatment. In addition, a biopsy should be performed if the PSA rises quickly and substantially. I recommend biopsy if the PSA rises by 1.0 ng/mL or more over one to two years, even if the actual number is less than 2.5 ng/mL. Thus, for example, I would recommend biopsy for a man whose PSA started at 0.6 ng/mL and one year later was at 1.7 ng/mL.

It is important to note that a high PSA or a rapid rise in PSA does not necessarily signify that cancer is present. It only means that the risk of cancer is high enough to merit a biopsy. In fact, in about 70 percent of these cases, the biopsy does not reveal cancer.

Testosterone Levels

Testosterone levels should be obtained early in the course of treatment to make sure that the dosage is appropriate. As discussed in

Chapter 6, the goal with gels and patches is to raise T concentrations well into the normal range, so I usually check blood levels within the first two to four weeks and make adjustments as necessary. Once a good T concentration is achieved, there is no need to check it more than once a year if all is going well.

For men receiving injection therapy, testosterone levels can be drawn either in the midportion of the cycle or just before the next injection. Again, once the appropriate dosage has been established, there is no need to check T concentrations in these men more than once per year unless there is some reason to believe that another adjustment is necessary.

For men using T patches or gels, blood tests to check T levels can be obtained anytime after the first one to two weeks. Men should not skip their usual testosterone application on the day of the blood test or else the result will appear to be too low.

Hematocrit and Hemoglobin

T therapy will increase the hematocrit and hemoglobin in most men. On average, the hematocrit rises by 3 percent, for example, from 42 percent to 45 percent. In most cases, the increase occurs within the first few months and then stabilizes once a new T level has been achieved. Larger increases in the hematocrit and hemoglobin tend to be seen in men using injections rather than transdermal treatments.

The hematocrit and/or hemoglobin should be checked at two to three months after beginning treatment, then once or twice more within the first year. After the first year, it is fine to check it annually.

What to Do If There Is Abnormality in the Hematocrit. Abnormalities of the hematocrit can mean that it is too low, which we call anemia, or too high, which we call erythrocytosis. Men with anemia should be evaluated by their regular physicians, because some cases, such as bleeding from the intestinal tract, can be serious. The most common causes are vitamin or iron deficiencies. However, for cases of anemia where there is no obvious cause, testosterone treatment itself can sometimes resolve the problem.

Another abnormality that can result directly from T therapy is an elevated hematocrit (or hemoglobin), called erythrocytosis. Mild elevations in the hematocrit require no treatment, but once the hematocrit rises above 54 percent (or hemoglobin rises above 18 g/dL), measures should be taken to lower the red blood cell count.

There are three choices to handle this situation:

1. Discontinue testosterone treatment until the hematocrit (or hemoglobin) normalizes
2. Decrease the dose of testosterone
3. Donate blood or have it drawn and discarded if it cannot be used by the blood bank (called therapeutic phlebotomy)

Bone Density

Because low T is associated with osteoporosis, which in turn can lead to fractures, it is important that men with low T have their bone density checked. It is a simple, noninvasive test that requires no more than five minutes to complete. Basically, the patient lies on a special table, the machine creates an image using extremely low-dose radiation (a fraction of a regular x-ray), and a computer determines the density of the bones. The hip and spine are the usual locations measured.

A bone density test should be obtained around the time T therapy is begun. If the bone density is normal, it should be repeated in two years. If the bone density is low, it should be repeated at one year. There is little point in repeating the test more frequently, because changes in bone density occur very slowly.

A relatively mild reduction in bone density is called osteopenia, while a more severe reduction is called osteoporosis. Osteopenia often does not require treatment, but it does require monitoring to make sure it does not become more severe. Testosterone therapy itself may be enough to normalize bone density over time in men with osteopenia. Osteoporosis is more serious and should be evaluated by someone knowledgeable in this issue. There can be important medical conditions other than low T that may cause osteoporosis, and more aggressive treatment is nearly always recommended to avoid the risk of fractures, especially in active or frail individuals.

Putting It All in Perspective

On the whole, T therapy is quite safe. Side effects or complications from treatment are uncommon and almost always will resolve if T therapy is discontinued. The most common risk of T therapy is development of an overly high red blood cell count, which is easily monitored and treated. Modern reevaluations of data regarding the greatest historical fears about T therapy—heart disease and prostate cancer—have provided reassuring results. Nonetheless, it is important that men receiving T therapy undergo regular health evaluation and monitoring, with particular attention paid to the prostate, hematocrit, and bone density.

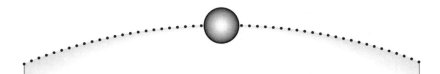

Questions and Answers

Q. *My doctor is afraid that testosterone therapy is dangerous for me because I have a strong family history of heart disease. Is this justified?*

A. No. T therapy is not dangerous for the heart. In fact, there is growing evidence that it may be helpful for cardiovascular health.

Q. *Will T therapy make hair grow on the palms of my hands?*

A. Only if you are a werewolf.

Q. *I'm afraid that if I take testosterone treatment, my sex drive will be out of control. I'm very happy in my marriage and wouldn't want to do anything that will endanger this by stupid behavior on my part. Should I be worried?*

A. No. Testosterone can improve or normalize libido. But it does not make men sex-crazed, at least not any more than they would have been with their own natural levels of testosterone. If you behave irresponsibly, the responsible party is you, not the testosterone.

Q. *Will I become bald if I use testosterone?*

A. No. Hair loss has not been associated with T therapy.

Q. *My doctor suggested I take testosterone for my symptoms of low T, but I've always found the muscle-bound look distasteful, and I don't want to look that way. How can I avoid looking like that?*

A. The muscle-bound look you dislike only comes from long hours in the gym, often accompanied by high-dose steroids. If you take testosterone as prescribed and exercise within reason, there is no need to worry about looking like Mr. America.

Q. *How do we really know that testosterone therapy is safe when there have been no long-term, large-scale studies on it? Isn't it possible that we may learn in ten or twenty years that T therapy increases the risk of certain diseases?*

A. It is always possible that in the future we may learn about a risk that we don't know about today. The reassuring thing about T therapy is that it has been around for a long time. So far there is no evidence that higher T levels are associated with any of the big medical problems, such as cancer or heart disease. There are now large numbers of men who have been on testosterone for as long as several decades without experiencing any apparent health risks. In fact, there is now evidence to show that men with normal T levels appear to live longer and with less heart disease than men with low T.

Chapter 9

Treating Men Who Have a History of Prostate Cancer

The oldest and most strongly held prohibition against testosterone therapy is its use in men previously diagnosed with prostate cancer. The fear has been that even in men who have been successfully treated for prostate cancer, raising testosterone levels will potentially make dormant, or sleeping, cancer cells wake up and start growing at a rapid rate. Thus, the FDA requires all testosterone products to include the warning that T therapy is contraindicated in men with a prior history of prostate cancer.

However, attitudes about this are changing—and changing rapidly—over just the last few years. The reasons for this are several, including the ongoing reevaluation of the old belief that raising the concentration of testosterone is to prostate cancer like pouring gasoline on a fire or feeding a hungry tumor. In addition, there is growing recognition that T therapy can provide important benefits to a man's quality of life, so the delicate medical balancing act between potential risk and possible benefit is shifting.

A major push for consideration of T therapy in symptomatic men with a history of prostate cancer has come from the large population of men who have been treated for prostate cancer over the last twenty-five years. Many of these men had small or low-grade cancers and, after treatment, were assured that they were cured and had no trace of any remaining cancer in their body. Despite having been given a clean bill of health, they were then told that they could not receive T therapy. As these prostate cancer survivors have questioned the basis for the T therapy prohibition, many physicians have been forced to reconsider whether the old arguments learned from their former teachers still make sense.

Felix was a sixty-six-year-old patient of mine who had undergone radical prostatectomy (the commonly performed operation to remove a cancerous prostate) ten years earlier. His prostate-specific antigen (PSA) blood test was undetectable, indicating no recurrence after all these years. But Felix was troubled by a complete lack of sex drive and felt tired all the time. Blood tests revealed a very low T level of 234 ng/dL. When Felix asked his urologist and oncologist whether his low T could be treated, both told him that T therapy was contraindicated because of his prior prostate cancer and warned him that T therapy might make his cancer come back.

"How does it make any sense," Felix asked, logically, "that they are afraid of prostate cancer growing uncontrollably when at the same time they tell me I don't have any cancer cells left in my body? If I don't have cancer cells, how could they grow?"

There are more and more men like Felix coming into their doctors' offices who have symptoms of low T and want to feel more normal. Over the last twenty-five years, we've seen an enormous increase in the number of men diagnosed and treated for prostate cancer. In fact, physicians have become so good at detecting these cancers early that at least 80 percent of men treated for prostate cancer can be considered true cures. So even if T therapy really did make prostate cancers grow, why couldn't these cured men receive treatment?

The entire prostate cancer story is somewhat confusing, even if we leave testosterone out of the picture for a moment. Here are some of the important facts. In the United States and in many other Western countries, prostate cancer is the most commonly diagnosed cancer, affecting over two hundred thousand American men each year. It is also the second most common cause of death in American males, with approximately thirty thousand men dying each year from this disease. Only lung cancer claims more lives among American men, although colon cancer now appears to be running neck and neck with prostate cancer for second place. That's the bad news. The good news is that mortality rates for prostate cancer in the United States have been declining for the last several years, presumably reflecting improvements in early diagnosis and treatment.

Here's one curious piece of the prostate cancer puzzle, though. Even before we had methods for early detection and before sophisticated treatments were widely available, only one in seven men diagnosed with prostate cancer actually died from it. This makes prostate cancer quite different from most other cancers, such as cancers of the lung, breast, colon, or pancreas, which usually progress fairly quickly without treatment. The explanation has been that prostate cancer is most frequently diagnosed later in life and tends to grow slowly, so that other medical conditions, such as heart disease, take a man's life before prostate cancer has a chance to do so—or even to cause symptoms. The slow growth of most prostate cancers has led to the medical aphorism that "Most men with prostate cancer die *with* the disease, but not *from* it."

With the introduction of the PSA blood test and the emphasis on early detection, more and more men are diagnosed with prostate cancer at a young age. Not only are they diagnosed, but they are also treated and cured at a relatively young age. When I was in medical training in the 1980s, at the beginning of the modern era of prostate cancer diagnosis and treatment, it was rare to see a prostate cancer patient who was younger than sixty-five years. Today, it is not unusual to diagnose men in their forties.

This early diagnosis and treatment has led to improved cure rates, but it also means that a sizable proportion of these cancer survivors have a reasonable expectation of living well for another twenty, thirty, or even forty years. Many of these men are in the baby boomer generation—an active group that has generally been unwilling to accept compromises to their quality of life.

This shift in age among men with a history of prostate cancer becomes highly relevant when one considers quality of life, as well as long-term risk. The balancing act between rewards and risks is entirely different for a fifty-five-year-old healthy man than for an eighty-five-year-old man with serious medical conditions, such as a bad heart. For the younger man, even a small long-term risk may be unreasonable, although improvement in quality of life over many years may be an important consideration.

For the eighty-five-year-old man, however, improved libido or a greater sense of vigor may seem less important (at least to his medical caregivers). On the other hand, if he really cares about it, does it make sense to deny him a potentially useful treatment based on a small or theoretical risk?

The argument reminds me of the joke about the ninety-nine-year-old man who comes to see a new doctor for the first time:

"Do you smoke?" asks the young doctor.

"I've been smoking two packs a day since I was sixteen," answers the old man.

"You've got to stop," replies the doctor. "Those things are going to kill you!"

In discussions with colleagues about testosterone and prostate cancer, the argument sometimes comes up that it takes perhaps thirty years or more for elevated testosterone levels to cause prostate cancer, to which I reply, "If that is true, then why do you fear giving testosterone therapy to men in their sixties and seventies?"

We are all concerned with risk, and rightly so. Yet it is important to put risk into perspective. What we choose for ourselves will often depend on our situation, such as age or health, and on the degree of risk. If T therapy caused all prostate cancer cells to grow rapidly and was associated with a high death rate within one year, no one would consider treatment, even in men we believe to be cured of cancer. The risk would simply be too great. The critical question is, how great is the risk? Unfortunately, this question has never been properly studied, so it is impossible to give any definite estimate regarding risk. However, there are several reasons to believe this risk is very low and perhaps even nonexistent. These reasons include recent studies in small numbers of men with a prior history of prostate cancer.

Recent Studies on T Therapy in Men with a History of Prostate Cancer

A number of physicians have told me that they have treated occasional patients with testosterone despite the fact that they'd been treated for prostate cancer in the past. The first people to publish their experience with doing this were Drs. Joel Kaufman and James Graydon, whose article appeared in the *Journal of Urology* in 2004.

In this article, Drs. Kaufman and Graydon described their experience in treating seven men with T therapy some time after these men had undergone radical prostatectomy as treatment for prostate cancer, with the longest follow-up being twelve years. None of the men had developed a recurrence of their cancer. Soon afterward, there was another paper by a group from Case Western Reserve University School of Medicine describing a similar experience in ten men with an average follow-up of approximately nineteen months. Then another group from Baylor College of Medicine reported the same results in twenty-one men.

In all these reports, not a single man out of the thirty-eight treated with testosterone developed a cancer recurrence. It is important to emphasize that all these reports included only men who were considered good candidates because they were at low risk of recurrence anyway. And in some cases, the duration of time the men received T therapy was relatively short. But it was reassuring that none of thirty-eight men who had suffered from prostate cancer in the past and who were treated for years with testosterone had developed a recurrence of prostate cancer.

This reassuring experience was bolstered by the published experience of Dr. Michael Sarosdy, who reported the results of T therapy in a group of thirty-one men who had received prostate cancer treatment in the form of radioactive seeds, called brachytherapy. This less-invasive form of treatment does not remove the prostate, so theoretically there is the possibility that a spot of residual cancer might still be present. With an average of five years of follow-up in these men, none of the thirty-one men had evidence of cancer recurrence.

The total number of men treated in these reports is still very small—much too small for anyone to be able to stand up and declare definitively, "Testosterone therapy is safe in men who have been treated for prostate cancer." But these reports have at least given us some perspective on the degree of risk of T therapy in men treated for prostate cancer. At a minimum, it is now possible to say that there is evidence from a number of small studies that T therapy in men who have been successfully treated for prostate cancer does not appear to be associated with a substantial risk of cancer recurrence over the first several years of treatment.

This is encouraging, as until recently it had been assumed almost universally that there was a substantial risk. These publications have provided support for physicians who are sympathetic to the requests of their patients requesting T therapy despite prior treatment for prostate cancer.

Relearning Old Lessons

"Those who cannot remember the past are condemned to repeat it."

—*George Santayana (1863–1952), U.S. philosopher*

One of the conceits of life that applies equally well to medicine is that modern beliefs and experiences are more relevant than events that occurred before our time. Thus, it is easy to discard or ignore lessons from the past. With prostate cancer, the modern era was born with the introduction of the nerve-sparing radical prostatectomy in 1982 and the PSA blood test a few years later. There was an incredible burst of new ideas and scientific articles around that time, and it has been easy to regard pre-1982 literature on prostate cancer as "old."

As I delved into the history of testosterone and prostate cancer (some of which I described in Chapter 7), I was amazed to find that between 1941 and 1981, there were multiple publications from several medical centers that described giving testosterone injections to men with prostate cancer. My amazement increased when I realized that nearly all these men already had metastatic disease.

This would be unheard of today! Whereas the recent reports I mentioned earlier involved only men who appeared *cured* of prostate cancer and were therefore at low risk for having any residual cancer cells that could potentially grow, these older reports involved only men who were known to have prostate cancer cells already growing within them. These were men at extremely high risk of dying if testosterone truly made their prostate cancers grow more rapidly. Clearly, the prohibition against giving testosterone to men with any hint of prostate cancer was not so well established then as it is today.

What happened to those men with metastatic prostate cancer who received testosterone? It turned out that there were two responses. Men who had already been castrated, with super-low testosterone concentrations, did poorly. The cancers really did act as if they were "happy" to be in the presence of testosterone again. But for men who had not been castrated, none of the studies showed much of a negative effect at all: none of the half-dozen studies I unearthed described any sudden worsening of prostate cancer in these men that could be attributed to testosterone. And nearly all of the reports indicated that at least some of the men felt better, with improved appetite, sense of vitality, and even reduced bone pain, which can be a major issue for men with metastatic prostate cancer. In other words, raising T in men with metastatic prostate cancer did not appear to cause any trouble, unless these men had previously undergone special treatment to deprive the tumor of almost all testosterone. How astonishing!

Now, I am not suggesting that men with metastatic prostate cancer should receive T therapy. Or even that these older studies prove that T therapy is safe in men who have been treated and hopefully cured of their cancer. The design of those older studies was not as rigorous as we would require today, and the tools for measuring growth or progression of prostate cancer were far less accurate as they predated the PSA test. So it cannot be said for sure that T injections did not cause any cancer growth in those men. Yet the lack of any obvious harm to those men with advanced cancer should provide some additional reassurance that normalizing testosterone in a man who appears cured of prostate cancer may not be such an outlandish idea.

More than fifty years after the first of these testosterone experiments, we seem to be relearning the same lessons. However, without an awareness of that period of medical history, it is as if we are performing the experiments for the first time.

Is It Safe for You to Take Testosterone?

If you have low T and you've already been treated for prostate cancer, you are probably wondering whether it is safe to take T therapy.

The short answer is that no one really knows. Safety is a tough issue to define, one we grapple with in medicine every day. How safe does something need to be in order to call it safe? If the risk was 1 in 10 that cancer would regrow, some might be willing to take the odds, but it's unlikely anyone would consider this degree of risk to be safe. But what if the risk was 1 in 100 or 1 in 1,000? What if the risk were fairly high that the cancer would regrow, but only after a delay of ten years or more? Would that make a difference? I'm making these numbers up, of course, because no one has yet performed studies that give us the answers. But the point is that in today's climate, the public and the medical establishment tends to treat *any* degree of risk as unsafe.

However, here is what I *do* know. Although there are many prostate cancer survivors with low testosterone, there are even more of these men with normal testosterone. And it has never been suggested to these men with normal testosterone that they should have their T levels brought down just enough to where they feel poorly!

Imagine two brothers, identical twins, who have both been treated for the exact same prostate cancer and have the same PSA. One feels good, is sexually active, and has a T level of 500 ng/dL. The other brother is always tired, has no libido, can't have sex, and has a T level of 200 ng/dL. When the second brother asks his doctor if he can have T therapy so he can feel better, the doctor says, "I'm sorry, but I can't do that. I'm afraid your cancer might come back."

To which the second brother responds, "I only want the same T level as my brother. Why is it safe for him to have a T level of 500 but not me? What's the difference? And if it's dangerous for me to have a T level of 500, let me go get my brother from the waiting room so you can lower his testosterone to my level!"

The reason we don't lower the first brother's T level to 200 ng/dL is that it doesn't make any difference. There is not a single study that has found any difference whatsoever in cancer outcomes for men with T concentrations of 200 ng/dL, or 500 ng/dL, or 800 ng/dL. The risk of T therapy in men with prostate cancer is theoretical, and the evidence I have cited here suggests that it may turn out not to be true. The limited evidence we have so far suggests that the risk, if it exists at all, is small.

A Remarkable Story

Let me share a remarkable story from my own practice. Warner was an eighty-four-year-old man who drove a considerable distance to see me for treatment of his sexual dysfunction. He was a gentleman's gentleman, with a bow tie, white hair, and upright carriage. He was extremely polite and still practiced law, going to the office every day. Warner had no sexual urge at all and hadn't had a decent erection in many years. "Could low testosterone be the cause?" Warner asked me.

Sure enough, Warner's T level was quite low. But on examination, I felt a very suspicious prostate nodule, and his PSA was considerably elevated at 8.5 ng/mL (normal is < 2.5 ng/mL). I performed a prostate biopsy, which revealed cancer.

The microscopic appearance of the cancer did not appear to be particularly aggressive. Warner and I discussed possible options, which included surgery, radiation, implantation of radioactive pellets in the prostate, or simply following his progress with regular examinations and PSA tests and deferring any real treatment unless there was evidence that the cancer was growing. I advised Warner that the microscopic appearance of the cancer suggested that the cancer might take many years to progress, although it was impossible to know this for sure.

"I don't want any treatment for the prostate cancer," Warner declared. "But I do want to see if testosterone improves my sex drive and erections. Will you treat my low testosterone?" he asked.

This was tricky for me. I explained to Warner that I had provided T therapy to a number of men who had been treated for prostate cancer and that none had developed any problems. Warner's situation was different, though. His prostate cancer was untreated. And it wasn't some tiny little tumor that had been discovered by accident, but a tumor that was associated with an elevated PSA. I told Warner that I had never given testosterone to anyone with untreated prostate cancer, nor did I know of any colleague who had done so. I explained that nearly all written materials considered T therapy to be absolutely contraindicated in his situation, and there was the possibility that his cancer could grow out of control with more testosterone.

"I'm willing to take the risk," Warner said, "if you're willing to treat me." I started Warner on T gel, and two weeks later his T level had risen well into the normal range at 645. At two months, he reported that he hadn't tried to do anything sexually yet, but he had definitely noted the return of sexual interest and was now awakening with morning erections, which had been absent for many years. "It's like having an old friend come back to see me again," he joked. On examination, the prostate was unchanged. His PSA was 8.7 ng/mL, a minor increase possibly due to his recent biopsy.

After six months of T therapy, Warner's PSA declined to 6.7 ng/mL. After eight months it was down to 5.7 ng/mL, and at ten months it was all the way down to 5.2 ng/mL. Incredible! Warner has now been treated with testosterone for more than two years. His most recent PSA has increased slightly to 6.2 ng/mL, a level that is still substantially lower than it was before T therapy. There is no evidence of cancer growth on examination.

Warner continues to be pleased with his T therapy, although his sexual function is not quite as good as he would like. And he is very pleased to have thus far avoided any treatment of his prostate cancer.

Warner was the first of my patients to start T therapy with known, untreated prostate cancer, but he was not the last. As more men choose to defer treatment of their cancer until it appears to be growing, this issue has come up again, and I have now treated a handful of men with T therapy despite untreated cancer. Although the follow-up on these men has been short, so far none of them has shown any evidence of cancer progression.

Final Thoughts on Testosterone and Prostate Cancer

If you've been diagnosed with prostate cancer, you're probably aware of the dizzying amount of conflicting information that is out there on the Internet and in various kinds of literature. You've also probably read that testosterone is dangerous for prostate cancer; if so, then I apologize for adding to the confusion.

I'd like to make a few final points to give some perspective on this story. First, it has become obvious that raising testosterone levels in a man with a history of prostate cancer is not like pouring gasoline on a fire. In fact, with the important exception of men who have undergone hormonal treatment to bring down their T levels to castrate levels, the limited evidence suggests that raising T levels does very little to the growth of prostate cancer.

Of course, one day new studies may suggest that there is a risk. However, no such study is likely to appear for at least five to ten years because it takes at least that long to judge whether a treatment has stimulated the growth of a cancer. Until then, we have to make decisions based on the available evidence, supported by logic and experience. For the moment, I am comfortable explaining to my patients that the use of T therapy in men with a history of prostate cancer entails an "unknown degree of risk" but that my assessment is that this degree of risk is small.

Second, it is important to recognize that even if you have low levels of testosterone as well as the symptoms of chronic fatigue, decreased libido, and erectile dysfunction, there is no certainty that raising T levels will alleviate your symptoms. There may be other reasons you are feeling this way. Moreover, there is no known benefit to T therapy if T levels are not truly low. Thus, the decision about whether to try T therapy requires balancing *possible* benefits with *possible* risks. This decision will be different for every man.

Third, T therapy is not itself a treatment for prostate cancer. Even though Warner's PSA dropped with T therapy, fluctuations in PSA values are common and no conclusions should be drawn from any one case.

Finally, it is important for any man with a history of prostate cancer to maintain his perspective on what is important to him. For some, it is enough to be alive and feeling reasonably well despite prostate cancer treatment. Adding a treatment that may stir up anxiety about their cancer may not be worth any benefit they may experience with regard to sex, mood, energy, or vitality. For others, the important thing is to live well. For them, an improved quality of life may be important enough to take on an unknown degree of risk, including a treatment that still lacks approval from the broader medical community.

In short, T therapy is not a cure-all or a solution to all of one's problems, and the decision to try T therapy is particularly complicated for men who have been treated for prostate cancer. The final chapter on the relationship of testosterone and prostate cancer has yet to be written, but so far, the ending appears to be far less scary than what has been assumed for the last several decades.

Attitudes are changing. For the last fifteen years, I've been asking for a show of hands at my lectures of those who would consider treating a man who appeared cured of cancer. Early on, it was rare for anyone to raise his or her hand. About seven to eight years ago, I started seeing one or two hands go up. And at a recent meeting of urologists, approximately 25 percent of those in attendance raised their hands, so these new ideas are beginning to take hold. It takes a while for new ideas to filter through a professional community, such as physicians, and the recent publication of the articles I mentioned earlier in the chapter has helped to refocus thoughts on this topic. I expect to see even more hands raised next year.

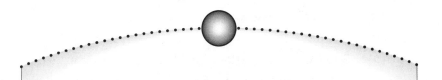

Questions and Answers

Q. *Is it true that men with higher levels of testosterone are more likely to have a recurrence of their prostate cancer?*

A. No. No one has published evidence that men with higher testosterone levels are at increased risk for any worrisome outcomes from prostate cancer.

Q. *My doctor told me that if I receive testosterone treatment, sleeping cancer cells in my body that have gone undetected until now might wake up and start to grow. Is this true?*

A. There is no evidence that T therapy will "awaken" cancer cells that weren't ready to "wake up" on their own. After all, most men already have substantial amounts of testosterone in their body anyway, even if the T levels in their bloodstream are low enough to cause symptoms. The one exception is the man who has already had his T levels reduced to almost zero by surgery or hormonal treatment. Apart from that one exception, no one has ever been able to show that raising T levels influences prostate cancer growth.

Q. *I had a radical prostatectomy two years ago to treat my prostate cancer, and the surgeon swore to me that he saved the nerves that are necessary for erection. Yet I've never had a single erection since the day of my surgery. Is it possible that testosterone treatment will restore my erections?*

A. The cause of your absent erections is almost certainly not hormonal. A very high percentage of men who undergo surgery for prostate cancer are unable to achieve adequate erections afterward, even if the nerves have been spared. Testosterone therapy is unlikely to improve the quality of erections when a man achieves no rigidity at all. However, it may be helpful if erections are present but diminished in quality. Before considering testosterone, though, you should explore the various standard treatments for erectile dysfunction, including pills, penile injections, or a penile implant.

Q. *After radiation treatment for my prostate cancer, my erections were fine for a year or so, but now they are almost gone. Is this a sign of low testosterone?*

A. Radiation treatment can cause delayed erectile dysfunction due to damage to the penile tissues. Low testosterone is a less common explanation, but it can also occur with radiation treatments. If you have additional symptoms of low T, such as a diminished libido or fatigue, you should have your T levels checked with a blood test.

Q. *My doctor agreed to prescribe testosterone to me even though I had surgery for prostate cancer five years ago. My PSA has been undetectable. How often should I have my PSA checked?*

A. I usually check the PSA and perform an examination every three months for the first year in a man with a prior history of prostate cancer. If nothing worrisome shows up in the first year, I will have the man come in at least twice yearly for an exam and the PSA blood test.

Q. *If what you write is correct, then why do so many physicians absolutely reject the idea of offering T therapy to a man after treatment for prostate cancer?*

A. It is difficult to let go of concepts we learned from our trusted teachers.

Q. *Do you think there will ever be a time when the average physician will consider offering testosterone to symptomatic men who have been treated for prostate cancer?*

A. Yes.

Chapter 10

The Future of Testosterone

Most of this book has been focused on helping men who might have low testosterone recognize their symptoms, learn how to have the diagnosis made, and obtain treatment. Right now, the world of T therapy for men with low T is all about symptoms or physical effects from low T, such as reduced bone density. But there is a larger story about testosterone that is only now developing and that may have far greater significance for men and their health. In this chapter, I will address the future of testosterone.

The key, far-reaching question that has yet to be answered is whether there might be important, long-term health benefits to having normal or even generous testosterone levels in our bodies. Much of the medical literature regarding testosterone over the last twenty years has been, in essence, playing defense. There have been so many concerns, myths, allegations, and scare stories about testosterone that the majority of what has been written and studied has been to determine whether testosterone is risky or safe. This emphasis on the potential risks or shortcomings of T therapy has distracted us from a larger question, namely, "Is a normal T level conducive to good health?" The short answer appears to be a qualified yes.

Throughout this book, I have shared positive stories from my patients about how T therapy has helped them with a variety of symptoms. Clearly, many men feel more energetic, vigorous, and alive with T therapy, not to mention having more interest in sex and improved sexual performance. These men feel better, enjoy their lives—and their partners!—more, and tend to have a better outlook on life. However, the most important question about testosterone is this: are men on T therapy *healthier* than untreated men with low T?

One of the sticky points in addressing this issue is how health is defined. For most of my patients who have responded nicely to T therapy, it would be a no-brainer to ask them whether they feel healthier—doesn't improvement in sexual function, energy, and strength represent better health? Yet from a broader perspective, the term *health* has little to do with symptoms and more to do with objective results that can be measured. When experts look at the effects of various lifestyle or medical practices on health, they often look at the effects on longevity and on the diseases that, in developed nations, are the most common causes of premature death: cardiovascular disease (heart disease and stroke) and cancer. How does having normal T levels stack up using this type of definition of health?

Testosterone and Longevity

To tackle the toughest issue first, testosterone has an interesting relationship to longevity. At least four studies published over the last several years have shown that men with high T levels appear to live longer than men with low T levels. The most dramatic of these studies was performed in a population of 858 veterans over forty years of age who were followed for an average of 4.3 years. In this study, the mortality rate (death rate) for men with testosterone levels of less than 250 ng/dL was 75 percent higher than men with normal T levels.

Another study performed in a geriatric rehabilitation unit found that men with low T levels died at a higher rate than men with normal T levels. A third study followed men with an average age of seventy-four years in the Rancho Bernardo community in California for 11.8 years. In this study, men whose T levels were in the lowest quarter of the population had a 40 percent increased risk of dying.

These are rather startling numbers, yet there seems to be little serious discussion at the upper levels of U.S. health policy about studying the potentially beneficial effects of T therapy on life expectancy. Although the veterans study did receive some short-lived media attention, no one is yet banging the drum to study the use of T therapy as a means of living longer.

To be fair, other studies have not found a relationship between testosterone and mortality. These negative studies have included healthier populations with a lower death rate, which may make it more difficult to show a difference based on T levels. Or perhaps T concentrations matter only in men who are at greater risk of dying because of age or illness.

These results that show a survival benefit for higher T levels are intriguing, but we are nowhere close to making any hard conclusions regarding the effect of T therapy on longevity. Even if we could say for sure that a normal T level is better than a low T level for long life, this still would not necessarily mean that T therapy would make a difference, because the studies did not look at the effects of raising T levels—they just investigated natural T levels in men. Perhaps men who died earlier had other reasons to also have low T, which was not picked up by the researchers. If this were the case, low T would just be an indicator of some other risk factor, and normalization of T levels would be unlikely to be helpful. This is all speculation, of course, but it certainly does make one wonder whether good T levels are beneficial for living a long life.

Testosterone and Cardiovascular Disease

What about the effect of T therapy on cardiovascular disease? As I've mentioned in previous chapters, there has been considerable work done to see whether high T levels might be bad for cardiovascular disease, and study after study has concluded that it is not. But what about the possibility that men with higher T levels might actually have a cardiovascular advantage over men with low T levels?

In the mortality studies I described previously, cardiovascular deaths were increased in the low T population in some studies, but not all. In addition, there are a number of studies that have shown that atherosclerosis, or thickening of the arteries, occurs at a higher rate in men with lower T than in men with higher T. The Rotterdam study, which I mentioned in Chapter 8, looked at calcifications in the aorta, and other studies have looked at the degree of thickening in the carotid arteries, which are the arteries that supply blood to the brain. These studies have shown that atherosclerosis is more likely to occur in men with low T and that men with higher levels of testosterone are more likely to have healthy blood vessels.

Recent data have shown a similar relationship between T concentrations and heart disease, which has created quite a stir. I've previously mentioned that one of the treatments for advanced prostate cancer is to reduce T levels almost to zero with medications. Although this treatment causes fewer men to die from their cancer, the new data indicate an increase in the number of deaths from heart disease among men treated in this way. A severe reduction in testosterone thus appears to be risky for blood vessels and the heart.

In addition, low T is associated with diabetes and obesity, as well as with a constellation of risk factors known as the metabolic syndrome. All of these increase the risk of cardiovascular disease, especially heart attacks. Thus low T is associated with a number of medical conditions that represent risk factors for cardiovascular disease.

As with longevity, though, this kind of association by itself is not enough to prove that T therapy would reverse those risks in men with low T. To prove this would require a very large, prospective study performed over many years to see what happens to men with low T who receive T therapy and to compare these men to others who receive only a placebo. No such study is even in the planning stages in the United States as of this writing, so we are left without hard evidence.

On the other hand, there are now quite a few studies that show that T therapy does reverse or improve some of the risk factors for heart disease—if not heart disease itself. For instance, T therapy in men with low T improves blood sugar control. And it reliably reduces the amount of fat in the body and waist circumference, each of which are risk factors for heart attacks. Finally, there is fascinating new evidence that T therapy has a beneficial effect on the metabolic syndrome, a set of indicators that predicts heart disease. These pieces of evidence do not yet mean that T therapy will reduce the risk of cardiovascular disease, but so far everything appears to be pointing in the right direction!

Testosterone and Cancer

Cancer is the other factor in terms of general health measures. This is an odd story, because there has been an unquestioned assumption for decades that higher testosterone is dangerous for prostate cancer. As I've discussed in detail in Chapter 7, there is little scientific evidence for this concern. In my view, the more intriguing question now is whether normal testosterone is safer than low T with regard to prostate cancer. Over the last ten years or so there has been evidence in humans to suggest that *low* T poses an increased risk of prostate cancer, as well as experimental evidence in animals that testosterone may be helpful in *controlling* prostate cancer growth.

Testosterone and Bone Health

It is now indisputable that testosterone is important for long-term bone health. We think of osteoporosis as a women's condition, but multiple studies show that men with low T are at increased risk of osteoporosis and fractures and also that T therapy improves bone density. Men may develop osteoporosis less frequently than women, but the effects can be just as devastating to men as they are to women.

Trending Positive

Sometimes the most telling piece of information is what has not been shown. In this case, a remarkable fact is that none of the types of studies I've mentioned have shown a worrisome impact of testosterone on major health areas. In an age where it is commonplace to hear news of conflicting study conclusions, even on the same day ("Coffee is good for you!" "Coffee is bad for you!"), we have not yet seen any major study come up with data suggesting that higher T levels have worrisome health effects.

So although there is not yet enough evidence to establish a consensus that testosterone is important for the big definition of health or that T therapy will make anyone live longer, there is already an abundance of data that seems to be pointing in a positive direction. I am certain that we will see much more on this topic over the coming ten years, including, hopefully, initiation of a large study to see the long-term effects of T therapy in terms of safety and overall health benefits. In the meantime, there is plenty of evidence to suggest that testosterone is good for one's health.

A Choice for Life

The biggest obstacle in addressing low testosterone and its treatment is not medical, but social. As I write these pages, the big story in the news is publication of a report revealing that many of the greatest baseball players in recent years have used testosterone or other steroids for performance enhancement. Too many of these media stories fail to distinguish the illicit and unethical abuse of testosterone by athletes from the legitimate, medical use of testosterone as therapy for men with low T.

We need to let go of the idea that testosterone is illegal, dangerous, and evil. It is not the cause of male violence or aggression. There is little evidence that it increases the risk of heart disease or prostate cancer; in fact, there is growing evidence that it may protect against these conditions. Men who use testosterone medications under their doctor's care as treatment for low T are not cheating or gaining some unfair advantage over coworkers whose T levels are normal. They are simply having their hormone levels restored to normal so that they can reach their full, normal potential.

There is nothing wrong with wanting to feel good, alive, vigorous, and connected to one's life. There is nothing wrong with wanting to feel upbeat, less cranky, and sharper mentally. There is nothing wrong with wanting to regain sexual intimacy with one's partner at any age or with being able to have a more normal and satisfying sexual experience.

What I hope for the future is that we can come to a place where T therapy for low T is seen as no different than treating deficiencies of other hormones. For instance, no one thinks there is anything wrong with treating an individual who has low thyroid hormone levels. Why should it be any different for low T?

Testosterone therapy does not bring clear benefits for everyone with low T. Even men with low T and every single known symptom may take T therapy and experience no benefit at all. And it is certainly possible that one day we will learn of an adverse effect of T therapy. But here is what is important about low T, based on what we know today:

- Low T is common and can affect men in many profound ways.
- Low T is easy to diagnose, based on symptoms and blood tests.
- There are several effective treatments to increase testosterone.
- Treatment improves symptoms in most, but not all, men with low T.
- After six decades of use, T therapy appears to be safe, with appropriate medical monitoring.
- There is evidence to suggest that a normal T level may be beneficial for health and long life.

We always have choices when it comes to our health. For many men with low T, learning about the condition and finding help to treat it is a good choice—a choice for life.

References

Agarwal PK, Oefelein MG. 2005. Testosterone replacement therapy after primary treatment for prostate cancer. *Journal of Urology* 173(2):533–36.

Araujo AB, Kupelian V, Page ST, et al. 2007. Sex steroids and all-cause and cause-specific mortality in men. *Archives of Internal Medicine* 167:1252–60.

Bhasin S, Cunningham GR, Hayes FJ, Matsumoto AM, Snyder PJ, Swerdloff RS, Montori VM. 2006. Testosterone therapy in adult men with androgen deficiency syndromes: An endocrine society clinical practice guideline. *Journal of Clinical Endocrinology and Metabolism* 91:1995–2010.

Bhasin S, Singh AB, Mac RP, Carter B, Lee MI, Cunningham GR. 2003. Managing the risks of prostate disease during testosterone replacement therapy in older men: Recommendations for a standardized monitoring plan. *Journal of Andrology* 24:299–311.

Bhasin S, Storer TW, Berman N, Yarasheski KE, Clevenger B, Phillips J, et al. 1997. Testosterone replacement increases fat-free mass and muscle size in hypogonadal men. *Journal of Clinical Endocrinology and Metabolism* 82:407–13.

Bremner WJ, Vitiello MV, Prinz PN. 1983. Loss of circadian rhythmicity in blood testosterone levels with aging in normal men. *Journal of Clinical Endocrinology and Metabolism* 56:1278–81.

Carpenter WR, Robinson W, Godley PA. 2008. Getting over testosterone: Postulating a fresh start for etiologic studies of prostate cancer. *Journal of the National Cancer Institute* 100:158–59.

Carter HB, Pearson JD, Metter EJ, et al. 1995. Longitudinal evaluation of serum androgen levels in men with and without prostate cancer. *Prostate* 27(1):25–31.

Cherrier MM, Craft S, Matsumoto AH. 2003. Cognitive changes associated with supplementation of testosterone or dihydrotestosterone in mildly hypogonadal men: A preliminary report. *Journal of Andrology* 24:568–76.

Dobs AS, Meikle AW, Arver S, Sanders SW, Caramelli KE, Mazer NA. 1999. Pharmacokinetics, efficacy, and safety of a permeation-enhanced testosterone transdermal system in comparison with bi-weekly injections of testosterone enanthate for the treatment of hypogonadal men. *Journal of Clinical Endocrinology and Metabolism* 84(10):3469–78.

English KM, Steeds RP, Jones TH, Diver MJ, Channer KS. 2000. Low-dose transdermal testosterone therapy improves angina threshold in men with chronic stable angina. *Circulation* 102(16):1906–11.

Gann PH, Hennekens CH, Ma J, et al. 1996. Prospective study of sex hormone levels and risk of prostate cancer. *Journal of the National Cancer Institute* 88(16):1118–26.

Greenstein A, Mabjeesh NJ, Sofer M, Kaver I, Matzkin H, Chen J. 2005. Does sildenafil combined with testosterone gel improve erectile dysfunction in hypogonadal men in whom testosterone supplement therapy alone failed? *Journal of Urology* 173(2):341.

Harman SM, Metter EJ, Tobin JD, et al. 2001. Longitudinal effects of aging on serum total and free testosterone levels in healthy men: Baltimore Longitudinal Study of Aging. *Journal of Clinical Endocrinology and Metabolism* 86(2):724–31.

Hoffman MA, DeWolf WC, Morgentaler A. 2000. Is low serum free testosterone a marker for high grade prostate cancer? *Journal of Urology* 163:824–27.

Hsing AW. 2001. Hormones and prostate cancer: What's next? *Epidemiologic Review* 23(1):42–58.

Huggins CB, Stevens RB, Hodges CV. 1941. The effects of castration on advanced carcinoma of the prostate gland. *Archives of Surgery* 43:209.

Hwang TI, Chen HE, Tsai TF, Lin YC. 2006. Combined use of androgen and sildenafil for hypogonadal patients unresponsive to sildenafil alone. *International Journal of Impotence Research* 18:400–4.

The Institute of Medicine. 2004. *Testosterone and aging: Clinical research directions.* Washington, DC: National Academies Press.

Kaufman JM, Graydon RJ. 2004. Androgen replacement after curative radical prostatectomy for prostate cancer in hypogonadal men. *Journal of Urology* 172(3):920–22.

Kupelian V, Page ST, Araujo AB, Travison TG, Bremner WJ, McKinlay JB. 2006. Low sex hormone binding globulin, total testosterone, and symptomatic androgen deficiency are associated with development of the metabolic syndrome in non-obese men. *Journal of Clinical Endocrinology and Metabolism* 91:843–50.

Lazarou S, Morgentaler A. 2005. Hypogonadism in the man with erectile dysfunction: What to look for and when to treat. *Current Urology Reports* 6:476–81.

Lazarou S, Reyes-Vallejo L, Morgentaler A. 2006. Wide variability in laboratory reference values for serum testosterone. *Journal of Sexual Medicine* 3:1085–89.

Marin R, Escrig A, Abreu P, Mas M. 1999. Androgen-dependent nitric oxide release in rat penis correlates with levels of constitutive nitric oxide synthase isoenzymes. *Biology of Reproduction* 61:1012–16.

Marks LS, Mazer NA, Mostaghel E, Hess DL, Dorey FJ, Epstein JI, Veltri RW, Makarov DV, Partin AW, Bostwick DG, Macairan ML, Nelson PS. 2006. Effect of testosterone replacement therapy on prostate tissue in men with late-onset hypogonadism: A randomized controlled trial. *Journal of the American Medical Association* 296:2351–61.

McNicholas TA, Dean JD, Mulder H, Carnegie C, Jones NA. 2003. A novel testosterone gel formulation normalizes androgen levels in hypogonadal men, with improvements in body composition and sexual function. *British Journal of Urology* 91:69–74.

Morgentaler A. 1999. Male impotence. *Lancet* 354:1713–18.

———. 2003. *The Viagra myth: The surprising impact on love and relationships.* San Francisco: Jossey-Bass/Wiley.

———. 2006. Testosterone and prostate cancer: An historical perspective on a modern myth. *European Urology* 50:935–39.

———. 2006. Testosterone and sexual function. *Medical Clinics of North America* 90:S32–34.

———. 2006. Testosterone replacement therapy and prostate risks: Where's the beef? *Canadian Journal of Urology* 13:S40–43.

———. 2006. Testosterone therapy for men at risk for or with history of prostate cancer. *Current Treatment Options in Oncology* 7:363–69.

———. 2007. Cultural biases and scientific squabbles: The challenges to acceptance of testosterone therapy as a mainstream medical treatment. *Aging Male* 10:1–2.

———. 2007. Guideline for male testosterone therapy: A clinician's perspective. *Journal of Clinical Endocrinology and Metabolism* 92:416–17.

———. 2007. Testosterone deficiency and prostate cancer: Emerging recognition of an important and troubling relationship. *European Urology* 52:623–25.

———. 2007. Testosterone replacement therapy and prostate cancer. *Urology Clinics of North America* 34:555–63.

Morgentaler A, Bruning CO III, DeWolf WC. 1996. Incidence of occult prostate cancer among men with low total or free serum testosterone. *Journal of the American Medical Association* 276:1904–6.

Morgentaler A, Crews D. 1978. Role of the anterior hypothalamus-preoptic area in the regulation of reproductive behavior in the lizard, Anolis carolinensis: Implantation studies. *Hormones and Behavior* 11:61.

Morgentaler A, Rhoden EL. 2006. Prevalence of prostate cancer among hypogonadal men with prostate-specific antigen of 4.0 ng/mL or less. *Urology* 68:1263–67.

Morley JE, Kaiser FE, Perry HM, et al. 1997. Longitudinal changes in testosterone, LH and FSH in healthy older men. *Metabolism.* 46(4):410–13.

Nieschlag E, Swerdloff R, Behre HM, Gooren LJ, Kaufman JM, Legros JJ, et al. 2005. Investigation, treatment and monitoring of late-onset hypogonadism in males: ISA, ISSAM, and EAU recommendations. *European Urology* 48:1–4.

Oh JY, Barrett-Connor E, Wedick NM, Wingard DL. 2002. Endogenous sex hormones and the development of type 2 diabetes in older men and women: The Rancho Bernardo study. *Diabetes Care* 25:55–60.

Pope HG Jr, Cohane GH, Kanayama G, Siegel AJ, Hudson JI. 2003. Testosterone gel supplementation for men with refractory depression: A randomized, placebo-controlled trial. *American Journal of Psychiatry* 160:105–11.

Rhoden EL, Estrada C, Levine L, Morgentaler A. 2003. The value of pituitary magnetic resonance imaging in men with hypogonadism. *Journal of Urology* 170:795–98.

Rhoden EL, Morgentaler A. 2003. Testosterone replacement therapy in hypogonadal men at high risk for prostate cancer: Results of 1 year of treatment in men with prostatic intraepithelial neoplasia. *Journal of Urology* 170:2348–51.

———. 2004. Risks of testosterone-replacement therapy and recommendations for monitoring. *New England Journal of Medicine* 350:482–92.

———. 2004. Treatment of testosterone-induced gynecomastia with the aromatase inhibitor, anastrozole. *International Journal of Impotence Research* 16:95–97.

————. 2006. Influence of demographic factors and biochemical characteristics on the prostate-specific antigen (PSA) response to testosterone replacement therapy. *International Journal of Impotence Research* 18:201–5.

Roddam AW, et al. 2008. Endogenous sex hormones and prostate cancer: A collaborative analysis of 18 prospective studies. *Journal of the National Cancer Institute* 100:170–83.

Sarosdy MF. 2007. Testosterone replacement for hypogonadism after treatment of early prostate cancer with brachytherapy. *Cancer* 109:536–41.

Shabsigh R. 2004. Testosterone therapy in erectile dysfunction. *Aging Male* 7:312–18.

Shores MM, Matsumoto AM, Sloan KL, Kivlahan DR. 2006. Low serum testosterone and mortality in male veterans. *Archives of Internal Medicine* 166:1660–65.

Shores MM, Moceri VM, Gruenwals DA, et al. 2004. Low testosterone is associated with decreased function and increased mortality risk: A preliminary study of men in a geriatric rehabilitation unit. *Journal of the American Geriatric Society* 52:2077–81.

Tenover JL. 1999. Testosterone replacement therapy in older adult men. *International Journal of Andrology* 22(5):300–6.

Traish AM, Toselli P, Jeong SJ, Kim NN. 2005. Adipocyte accumulation in penile corpus cavernosum of the orchiectomized rabbit: A potential mechanism for veno-occlusive dysfunction in androgen deficiency. *Journal of Andrology* 26:242–8.

Vermeulen A, Verdonck L, Kaufman JM. 1999. A critical evaluation of simple methods for the estimation of free testosterone in serum. *Journal of Clinical Endocrinology and Metabolism* 84:3666–72.

Wang C, Swerdloff RS, Iranmanesh A, et al. 2000. Transdermal testosterone gel improves sexual function, mood, muscle strength, and body composition parameters in hypogonadal men. *Journal of Endocrinology and Metabolism* 85(8):2839–53.

Whitsel EA, Boyko EJ, Matsumoto AM, Anawalt BD, Siscovick DS. 2001. Intramuscular testosterone esters and plasma lipids in hypogonadal men: A meta-analysis. *American Journal of Medicine* 111(4):261–68.

Zvara P, Sioufi R, Schipper HM, Begin LR, Brock GB. 1995. Nitric oxide mediated erectile activity is a testosterone dependent event: A rat erection model. *International Journal of Impotence Research* 7:209–19.

Index